# MORE
# PUZZLES, PARADOXES
# AND BRAIN TEASERS

# MORE PUZZLES, PARADOXES AND BRAIN TEASERS

*Stan Gibilisco*

**TAB BOOKS Inc.**
Blue Ridge Summit, PA

FIRST EDITION
FIRST PRINTING

**Library of Congress Cataloging-in-Publication Data**

Gibilisco, Stan.
   More puzzles, paradoxes and brain teasers / by Stan Gibilisco.
      p.   cm.
   Includes index.
   ISBN 0-8306-9095-6      ISBN 0-8306-3295-6 (pbk.)
   1. Mathematical recreations.   I. Title.
QA95.G478   1989
793.7'4—dc20                                    89-35336
                                               CIP

TAB BOOKS Inc. offers software for sale. For information and a catalog, please contact TAB Software Department, Blue Ridge Summit, PA 17294-0850.

Questions regarding the content of this book should be addressed to:

**Reader Inquiry Branch**
**TAB BOOKS Inc.**
**Blue Ridge Summit, PA 17294-0214**

Acquisitions Editor: Roland S. Phelps
Editor: Lisa A. Doyle
Production: Katherine Brown

# CONTENTS

# Introduction

Here is a collection and discussion of some more puzzles and paradoxes in the mathematical and physical universes. There was considerable interest generated by my first book in this series, *Puzzles, Paradoxes, and Brain Teasers,* prompting me to write about more bizarre problems and phenomena. And there is more to come.

The book begins with some popular and also some lesser-known tricks and baffling realities of mathematics and physics. These are things you can try out on friends at parties, but some of them are more appropriate for figuring out in the library on a day when there isn't much else to do. Such puzzles and paradoxes can begin as a diversion and then evolve to ends in themselves.

Some of the more famous, long-standing problems are then examined such as angle trisection, the Parallel Postulate, and Fermat's Last Theorem. The third chapter acknowledges that humans have always sought refuge in the notion that there must be something absolute in the universe—and looks at the aspects of this problem.

What causes what? Can the future dictate what has already happened in the past? By certain reasoning, yes. Chapter 4 goes into how this might be possible according to some models of space-time events. Chapter 5 asks why do things occur in bunches? Why do baseball teams have "streaks"? Why do athletes "plateau"and then dramatically improve suddenly?

The question of the paranormal, supernatural, metaphysical, or occult world gets into tabloids with great regularity. People like to read about things involving mind-over-matter power, immortality, and thought communication. Perhaps the intrigue in these things is because they are fun to think about. Perhaps there is a deeper reason. Science and metaphysics seem to repel each other; the scientist runs the risk of ridicule by pursuing research in this field, and those published materials that have any positive conclusions are often poisoned by lack of objectivity and downright sensationalism. Chapter 6 takes a passing glance—albeit a long glance—at this phenomenon and the ways in which related experiments are conducted.

A recent branch of science, fitting into neither pure mathematics nor pure physics, is called the science of *chaos*. It is gaining popularity as a field of research. Chapter 7 discusses how the phenomena that actually occur in this universe of ours are sometimes so baffling that we can explain them only by proving that we cannot explain them—not fully, at least. This realization is part of the new science. Other books written on this subject are bestsellers because the subject of chaos deals with the true nature of things—infinitely complicated and unpredictable.

Suggestions for puzzles, paradoxes, and brain teasers for future editions are welcome. Meanwhile, have a paradoxical day.

# CHAPTER 1

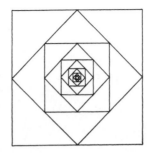

# Games and Puzzles

T HERE ARE MANY MATHEMATICAL GAMES AND PUZZLES THAT CAN BE USED FOR ENTER-
tainment on occasions when boredom seems to fill up the mind as if it were water
finding its own level. Such games don't cost anything (and, in fact, you can make money
by betting on some of their outcomes if you are sufficiently shrewd and broke and don't
care if the vice squad comes and has you arrested and imprisoned for gambling). This
chapter is an assortment of such games, puzzles, and amusements—all of which really
should be common knowledge and required learning in our public grade schools.

## Tic-Tac-Toe

This game must have some profound significance, cosmic overtones, or deep mean-
ings. It can be found along with such famous quotations as "Kilroy was here" and such
emotional symbols as the "peace" sign on subway walls and in restroom stalls. Such
games are often incomplete, indicating how easily humans give up hope when victory is so
near. They also might be incomplete to indicate a "draw"—a condition that, if the game is
properly played, the player making the second move should always be able to achieve in
the end, even if the first player is more brilliant than Goethe.

It is often said that the best initial move, if you happen to be the lucky player who gets
to mark first, is to take the center square, because there are eight possible places to place
your symbol after that in your quest to obtain three in a row. Anyone who moves first and
does *not* do this is automatically suspect; if you're gambling on tic-tac-toe and your opponent as a starter places his/her mark in one of the corner squares, he or she is probably
rather dull; if your opponent takes one of the side squares, it's a good sign that you'll
shortly be wealthier and you should have bet for more money.

In Fig. 1-1, assuming that the X player moves first, the possible counter moves for the
O player (for obtaining an eventual draw) are illustrated. At A, it is assumed that the X
player is halfway intelligent and has taken the center square. The the O player must take a

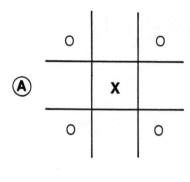

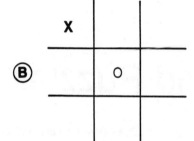

Fig. 1-1. Moves for the second (O) player for obtaining an eventual draw in tic-tac-toe. At (A), X takes center; at (B), X takes corner; at (C), X takes a side square.

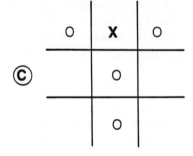

corner square. At B, the X player has taken a corner square first. Then, the O player must take the center. At C, if the X player takes a side square, there are four other possible moves for the O player.

Since there is only one possible O move to result in a draw if X takes a corner square first (whereas there are four possible O moves if X takes the center first), you might conclude that it is actually smartest for the starting player to take a corner square. The argument for the center is based simply on its being the focal point for the greatest number of victories. Actually, however, although a draw can be more easily guaranteed by taking a corner square, a victory could be more likely by taking the center square. This involves psychological concepts that can't be put into mathematical form very well.

While on the subject of psychological things, let's put this question out: In tic-tac-toe, what is the probability that the first player will put down an X rather than an O? It is certainly *not* 50-50. People are much more likely to start with X, just as when counting off by twos, people almost always start with "one." Mathematically, it isn't necessary to put down X first or to begin with "one" in these cases. But it seems to be a social convention. Perhaps it is in some obscure etiquette book that these things are socially dictated. I can see it even now, neatly printed on the page in the chapter "Games" under "T" (tic-tac-toe, rules of conduct). You might try throwing people sometime by starting with O rather than X; if you really want to get attention, the next time you are in a group that is going to divide into two subgroups, start the count with "two."

## The Illusion of the Tall Glass

This is a good way to win small bets at bars or other occasions where people are so saturated with triviality that games of this nature can capture complete attention.

Find a tall tumbler, cylindrical in shape (not wider at the top than at the bottom or vice versa). It should be tall enough so that upon casual observation, almost anyone would conclude that the height is greater than the circumference. You should have a piece of string or other flexible but not stretchable measuring barometer with you, so that you can demonstrate your claim. It's a very good bet that the circumference is greater than the height of a tumbler, even when, at first glance, it seems impossible that this could be true.

Of course the diameter, not the circumference, is what most perceive when looking at a tumbler in an attempt to discern how big around it is. The circumference is equal to about 3.14 times the diameter. Visualize *that*, such as placing three tumblers mentally side-by-side and adding a little bit extra, and this will give you a somewhat more accurate picture. Even then, however, remember that the eye/brain apparatus has, for some reason, evolved with a propensity for exaggerating the vertical and reducing the magnitudes of horizontal displacements. So even if you do place three of the tumblers together and imagine another 0.14 of them alongside, you will not get a mentally accurate picture of the situation. Your eye/brain will still tend, if you are like most people, to emphasize the height of the tumbler over the 3.14 diameters.

Note—You should always check this out first, with various tumblers, before performing this trick in a bar and risk losing money. (Don't come crying to me if you haven't taken the necessary precautions.)

## Expansion of a Bridge

All bridges more than a few feet long have devices to accommodate the expansion and contraction caused by temperature changes. This little trick should make it quite apparent how important these gaps really are.

Suppose a bridge is a mile long. Let's imagine a suspension bridge, so that the situation is made more real (a bump actually will develop in a suspension bridge, whereas a supported bridge might just crack and break apart). This bridge is shown in Fig. 1-2A.

Now suppose that it gets hot and the bridge gets three feet longer because of the expansion. While it is not difficult to install gaps that total three feet over a mile-long span, let's suppose the engineers have failed to do this. Suppose further that the expansion occurs so as to make the center of the bridge rise, with the half-mile sections on either side of the center remaining straight (Fig. 1-2B). What is the height of the bump, h, in the middle of the bridge after the three-foot expansion?

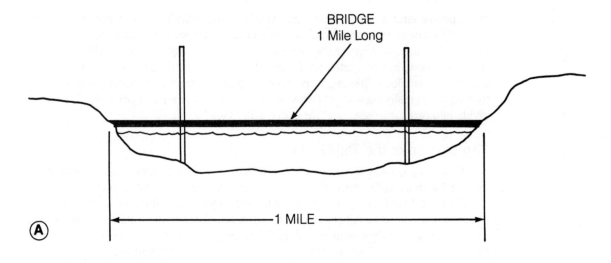

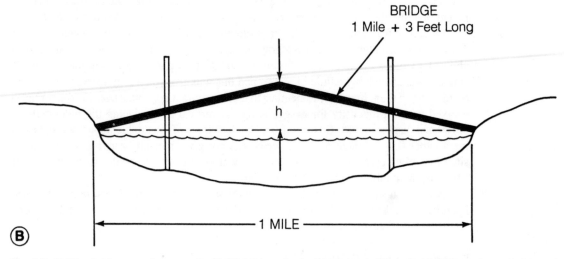

**Fig. 1-2.** At (A), a bridge spanning one mile. At (B), bridge after having expanded three feet, creating a bump in the center. How high is the bump?

Calculate the answer according to the diagram of Fig. 1-3. The height $h$ forms one side of a right triangle. The base of the triangle is $1/2$ mile or 2640 feet. The hypotenuse is 2640 + 1.5 feet (half of the 3-foot expansion) or 2641.5 feet. If the base is denoted as side $A$ and the hypotenuse by side $B$, then from the Pythagorean theorem:

$$A^2 + h^2 = B^2$$

and therefore that

$$
\begin{aligned}
2640^2 + h^2 &= 2641.5^2 \\
h^2 &= 2641.5^2 - 2640^2 \\
&= 6977522.25 - 6969600 \\
&= 7922.25
\end{aligned}
$$

and therefore

$$h = \sqrt{7922.25} = 89 \text{ feet (approximately)}$$

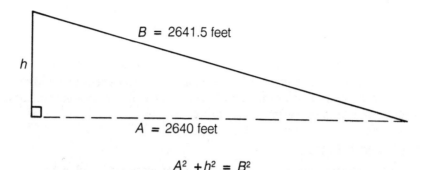

$$A^2 + h^2 = B^2$$

**Fig. 1-3.** Right-triangle geometry for solving problem of the bridge.

This should come as a surprise. Most expect, intuitively, that the bump would be much smaller than that. Actually, however, driving over the bridge with the 89-foot bump would not feel much different than driving over it with no bump. This is simply because the bump is so flattened out over the span of the bridge. In this sense, then—the practical sense—our intuition is correct; the bump is practically unnoticeable. The actual passing over the center of the bridge would be attended by only the most minor jostle, because the angle at the bump would be nearly 180 degrees (flat) even though the bridge is 89 feet higher than it should be at that point.

## The Result Is Always . . .

Perhaps you have heard number tricks where the result is always a certain number, or is always the number you started with. This trick is easy to figure out if you consider the problem backwards. In fact, you can make up your own such problems backwards, and then reverse all of the steps to get the "mystery."

Here is a simple example. Start with any integer $n$, and multiply it by 10. Then divide by the original number, and subtract 10. The result is always zero. This puzzle was made up simply by starting with the number desired at the end, in this case zero. Then 10 was added to it. This results in a sum of 10. Now multiply 10 by an arbitrary integer $n$, getting $10n$. Dividing by 10 gives $n$—the "arbitrary" number, and the number you can start the original "mystery" with.

You can invent more complicated tricks using this same scheme. Select some number that you want to always end up with, and work on it, using the arbitrary integer $n$ at one or more points along the way. You can make puzzles sufficiently complicated so that people will not be likely to see through them as easily as this example can be resolved.

Here is an example that is a little harder. Start with any integer $n$, and add 2. Multiply this result by 3. Then subtract 6 from the result. Finally, divide by $n$. The final number is always 3. You can verify this with an algebraic demonstration of the process in reverse. The only catch here is that $n$ cannot be zero because one of the steps is to divide by $n$.

5

For example, if $n = 1$,

$$1 + 2 = 3$$
$$3 (1 + 2) = 9$$
$$3 (1 + 2) - 6 = 3$$
$$\frac{3 (1 + 2) - 6}{1} = 3$$

The secret to all of these tricks, where a certain digit is obtained at the end of a process, involves the cancellation of the initial value $n$ so as to render a certain constant. When you reverse the process, this is easy to see.

## Problems with Liars

There are numerous brain teasers that involve that species of people who always lie. These people are not pathological liars, but they have indeed found a sense of absolute truth in that they know and verbalize exactly what that truth is *not*, without ever making a mistake.

In one particular country there are two species of people: one species tells the truth, and the other always lies. Suppose you have lived in this country, and because both species of natives look and dress too much alike for you to be able to tell the difference, you decide you want to leave. This requires only that you find the correct route to get out of there.

You come to a fork in the road and there, calmly sitting on a tree stump and smoking a corncob pipe, is a native. You are unable to tell if this native is a truth-teller or a liar, but you are anxious to get out of the country. How can you ensure that you will get on the right road, knowing not which one will lead you out, by asking this native? You cannot simply ask, "Which road leads out of the country?" because if the native is lying, he'll put you on the road that leads back in. But there is a question—in fact, there are several different questions—you can ask, and you will be able to get yourself on the right path whether the native is a truth-teller or liar.

Suppose you point to the road leading off toward the right, and ask the native, "If I were to ask you if this road leads out of the country, would you tell me yes?"

If the native says, "yes" it means he would in fact say "yes" if he were a truth-teller, and you would have pointed to the correct road. If he says "yes" and he is a liar, that means he is lying about the fact that he'd really tell you "no." But he would tell you "no" if you had pointed to the correct road and simply asked, "Does this road lead to the border?" Thus, if the native answers "yes" to your complex question, you have pointed to the road you want, regardless of the truth-telling ability of the person. There is the assumption here that the native really knows which road is which. If the native were ignorant he might answer "yes" without knowing anything about the roads at all. But the people of this country, while either purely truth-tellers or purely liars, are not stupid. They know the true answer to every question.

A variation of the truth-teller/liar problem is perhaps the more familiar "This statement is false." This can be expanded into larger groups of statements. One example is an index card on the front of which is printed, "The statement on the other side is true."

Eager to know what this great truth might be, the victim flips the card over to find: "The statement on the other side is false."

Suppose there are four statements as follows:

(1) One statement among these is false.
(2) Two statements among these are false.
(3) Three statements among these are false.
(4) Four statements among these are false.

How many of the statements are actually false? Assume that if a statement contradicts itself, it is false.

You can proceed according to combinatorial process. The statement (4) must be false, because it contradicts itself (if all four statements are false, then D is false, and this means D is true, a contradiction). From then on, you are invited to show that only statement (3) is true. Any other combination creates contradictions.

## The Missing Dollar

Three people go out to supper and end up spending 51 dollars total. Each person gives the waitress 17 dollars. They are regular customers and the owner of the restaurant decides to let them have their drinks on the house, so he sends them back 5 dollars. He gives this 5 dollars to the waitress to return to the customers. The waitress gives each customer just 1 dollar, keeping 2 for herself. Thus each of the people had actually paid 16 dollars for a total of 48 dollars. The waitress has 2 dollars. The total sum is therefore 50 dollars.

What happened to the extra dollar?

Problems like this are exceptionally frustrating for certain people. Tell this to some people next time you take them to dinner—especially if they are giving you a hard time about something.

Of the original 51 dollars, the manager kept 46 dollars. The waitress kept 2 dollars. The customers each got a dollar back. The total sum mentioned in the brain teaser has nothing to do with the sum in the actual transaction.

## A Geometric Fallacy

Recently I got an inquiry regarding a square, 6 units on a side, that could be transformed into a rectangle 7 by 5 units, thus creating a missing square unit. I couldn't find anything with that particular number of units, but here is a similar problem.

In Fig. 1-4A, a square is divided into 64 square units, 8 on a side, and then is cut along the indicated lines, making two right triangles measuring 3-by-8 units, and two irregular trapezoids consisting of 3-by-6 rectangles added to 2-by-5 right triangles. These four pieces are rearranged to create a 13-by-5 rectangle (Fig. 1-4B).

The rectangle has 65 square units.

How is this possible? Where does the extra square unit come from? If you look closely at Fig. 1-4B, the problem is in the center of the rectangle. There are two 1-by-3 right triangles there. Just to the left and right, as shown in the drawing of Fig. 1-4C, there are two 2-by-5 right triangles. This is not the same ratio as 1 by 3. So the long diagonal line going down the large rectangle cannot be straight. This is how the extra area gets added in. It occurs over such an elongated shape that it is difficult to discern.

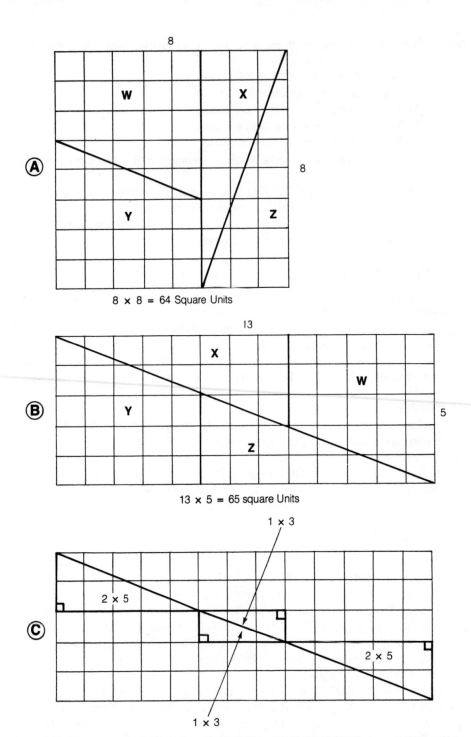

8

W          X

(A)                                              8

Y          Z

8 x 8 = 64 Square Units

13

X

(B)          Y                                    5

Z

13 x 5 = 65 square Units

1 x 3

2 x 5

(C)

2 x 5

1 x 3

**Fig. 1-4.** At (A), a square is divided into parts W, X, Y and Z. At (B), the parts are reassembled into a rectangle with an area one square unit larger than that of the square. At (C), illustration of the flaw in the puzzle.

## Pennies and Nickels

Suppose you have three pennies and three nickels, and three matchboxes in which to put them. You label the boxes PP, NN, and PN, standing for penny penny, nickel nickel and penny nickel. You intend to place the coins into the boxes in sets of two, according to this scheme.

But once you have put the coins in the boxes, you realize that you have not put the right pairs of coins into the right boxes. You know that one box contains two pennies, one box contains two nickels, and one box contains a penny and a nickel—but the labeling for each box is wrong. So you will have to change the labels.

You don't want to repack the boxes. But you can discover the correct labeling for the boxes by picking just one coin from one box. From which box should you pick a coin in order to do this?

Simply draw a coin out of the box labeled PN. If it is a penny, then there must be another penny in the box (if it was a nickel, the label would be correct, but remember that all three boxes are labeled wrong). Therefore, change the box labeled PN to PP. The box labeled PP must thus have two nickels in it. The box labeled NN must have a penny and a nickel. Similar reasoning applies if a nickel is taken from box PN.

## Tricks with Coins

Place two coins as shown in the drawing of Fig. 1-5. They can be any type of coin, as long as they are the same denomination (and thus the same diameter). Place one directly above the other, and they should both be right side up, with the images on both coins in the same attitude.

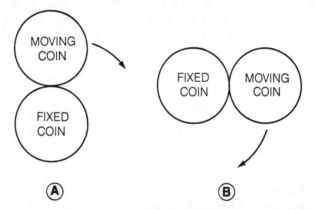

Fig. 1-5. Rolling a coin around another coin. At (A), starting position, both coins right side up and with their images at the same attitude. At (B), after one-quarter revolution.

Now, roll the top coin around the bottom coin in a clockwise direction. The top coin will end up on the bottom after it has gone halfway around. How many rotations of the coin are made when it revolves halfway around? Try this and see.

Here is another trick, requiring three pennies, to be initially set up as shown in Fig. 1-6. Call the pennies A, B, and C. How can you place C between A and B without *moving* B and without *touching* A in any way (or blowing on any of the coins)?

9

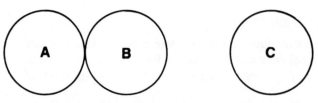

Fig. 1-6. Arrangement of three coins for repositioning as discussed in text.

If you are acquainted with physics, this should be easy to solve. All you have to do is hold coin B down firmly and propel coin C towards B so that C strikes B while you are not touching C. This will cause a shock wave to travel through coin B, throwing coin A away from coin B. It is then an easy task to move coin C so that it is between A and B.

How many pennies must you stack up vertically (one on top of the other, making a cylindrical pile) so that the height of the pile is equal to the diameter of one penny? Try this and see. The result may surprise you. Try the same experiment with other coins.

Coin flipping is a well-known pastime; every football game starts with a coin toss to determine who will get to choose whether they want to kick off or receive. The probability of "heads" (H) and "tails" (T) is assumed to be 50-50. If a coin is flipped twice, there are four possible outcomes: HH, HT, TH and TT. If a coin is flipped three times, there are eight ways the sequence can occur: HHH, HHT, HTH, HTT, THH, THT, TTH and TTT. The chances of each of these sets of flips is, in general, $1/2^n$ where $n$ is the number of flips. Consequently, there is a one in eight or 12.5-percent chance of getting THT when a coin is flipped three times.

However, there are certain ways to make it an unbalanced bet. If a person calls a certain combination of three tosses, you can always increase your chances of getting the correct combination to greater than 12.5 percent. The secret is to take the last call and eliminate it; then reverse the second call and place it ahead of the remaining two. For example:

| | |
|---|---|
| HTH | is called |
| HT | drop third call |
| HHT | place opposite of second call ahead of sequence |

The odds of your being correct are greater than 12.5 percent. This was in fact proven by a mathematician, W. Penney. You can list the various transformations that result from the foregoing process:

| | | |
|---|---|---|
| HHH | becomes | THH |
| HHT | becomes | THH |
| HTH | becomes | HHT |
| HTT | becomes | HHT |
| THH | becomes | TTH |
| THT | becomes | TTH |
| TTH | becomes | HTT |
| TTT | becomes | HTT |

The probabilities of these transformations can be calculated as being 1 in 7 for HHH into THH and for TTT into HTT; 1 in 3 for HHT into THH and for TTH into HTT; and 1 in 2 for the remainder of the transformations. In all cases, the chances are better than 1 in 8, the probability of being correct for purely guessing.

## A Bet You Can't Lose

Ask someone for a 5-dollar bill. Place this bill, along with a five of your own, into your pocket (making sure there isn't any other money in the pocket you choose). Offer the person the entire contents of your pocket (in dollars) for 7 dollars.

This doesn't sound like a bad deal. The guy shells out 7 dollars and receives 10 in return. This is the way it might seem at first thought until the poor soul realizes he's purchased 10 dollars in return for 12 (he had already given you 5). It helps if the person you're fooling in this situation has had a few drinks.

## Proving −1 = 1

There are various ways to prove that −1 is equal to 1. All such "proofs" involve oversights of one form or another. A common method is this:

$$\sqrt{-1} = \sqrt{-1}$$
$$\sqrt{1/-1} = \sqrt{-1/1}$$
$$\sqrt{1}/\sqrt{-1} = \sqrt{-1}/\sqrt{1}$$
$$\sqrt{1}\sqrt{1} = \sqrt{-1}\sqrt{-1} \text{ (Cross-multiplication)}$$
$$\sqrt{1}^2 = \sqrt{-1}^2$$
$$1 = -1$$

There at first appears to be nothing wrong with any of the steps in this process. However upon closer examination, when speaking of $\sqrt{1}$, don't neglect the fact that there are two values that satisfy this expression: 1 and −1. Similarly, $\sqrt{-1}$ has two solutions, the imaginary $i$ and its negative, $-i$. When you consider that $\sqrt{1} = \pm1$ and $\sqrt{-1} = \pm i$, then the difficulties evaporate, and you find yourself proving that $\pm1 = \pm1$. This is of course quite true, although it is unclear how we are to deal with numbers that may take more than one value "at the same time."

Other "proofs" that have obviously false results can involve such subtleties as division by zero:

$$x = 0$$
$$x(x - 1) = 0$$
$$x - 1 = 0 \qquad \text{(divide by } x\text{)}$$
$$x = 1$$
$$1 = 0$$

The problem here is that the third step divides both sides of the equation by $x$, but the first step stated that $x = 0$. More subtle ways of doing this have been devised. Of course, if 1 = 0, then 1 = −1 by applying this fact twice in a row. Then all of the integers are equal to each other, and the rational numbers are reduced to triviality.

## The Principle of Indifference

One common principle that is applied to events in calculating their probabilities is called the *principle of indifference*. If there are $n$ events and there is no reason to believe that any of them are more likely to happen than any other, then if one event occurs, the chances of its being a previously chosen one are $1/n$. Another way of putting this is as follows. Let possible events be called $x_1, x_2, x_3, \ldots x_n$. Then the probability of event $x_i$, where $i$ is an integer from 1 to $n$ inclusive, taking place with a single sampling is equal to $1/n$ (or $100/n$ percent) if there is no reason to think that the choices are weighted in any way.

This seems simple enough—although a previous section in this chapter demonstrated one case where coin tosses are actually weighted when it would seem they are not. People often make this mistake, thinking that probabilities are not weighted when they actually are in various scientific endeavors. You might wonder for example what the probability is that there is life on the planet Saturn. Whatever you decide the chances are, don't neglect one fact: the odds are weighted all the way—either 0 or 100 percent. Either there *is* life on Saturn or there *isn't*. What you believe has nothing at all to do with it.

Less extreme examples are plausible. "What is the probability that someone will swim the 100-meter freestyle in under 46.5 seconds by the year 2000?" "What are the chances of the Russians getting to Mars before the United States?" Anyone who attempts to answer these questions may have real data to draw upon, but after the facts, they will be meaningless. Either the events in question will have occurred, or they won't have. And what you have in mind about it now probably bears no relation to this outcome. It is clear that basing probabilistic calculations on our beliefs is a dangerous business. But getting back to the principle of indifference as it applies to situations where our beliefs are (to us) well founded, imagine taking four playing cards, two red and two black, and shuffling them up and laying them all in a row face down. Then pick two of the cards at random. What is the probability that the two cards are the same color?

This problem can be approached as follows: Assume that the chances of a card being either red or black are 50-50. There are four cards, so the possible combinations are black and black, red and black, black and red or red and red. It would seem reasonable to suppose that each of these combinations is 1 in 4 (25 percent) likely, and that the chances of the cards being the same color are 1 in 2 (50 percent). Matching colors represent two of the four combinations. If you reason this way, you are mistaken.

Look at it another way. There are three possibilities. Either both of the cards are red, both are black, or one is red and one is black. These are three different cases and you might say that the chances of getting matching colors must therefore be 2 in 3 (66.66 . . . percent. This, too, is wrong.

Try looking at it this way. When you pick a card, it is either red, or else it is black, and the chances are 1 in 2 (50 percent) for either color. If you have picked a red card, there are two black and one red remaining. If you have picked black, there are two red and one black left. When you pick the second card, then, you must pick the one of three that is the same color as the first one that you picked. Hence your chances of getting matching colors ought to be 1 in three (33.33 . . . percent). *This* is the correct way to look at the problem.

Here is another misapplication of the principle of indifference. Suppose you take a piece of paper and draw a circle on it, and you tell a friend that this circle has a diameter not less than 2 inches nor more than 4 inches. What is the probability that the diameter is between 2 and 3 inches compared with the chances of it being between 3 and 4 inches? Suppose that you are not psychologically in favor of smaller or larger objects, so your preferences do not affect the size of the circle, except for the already-agreed-on limits.

The answer depends on how you are to determine the size of the circle. This can be done in terms of its diameter, as is implied by the problem; but there is another way, and that is according to its interior area. If you determine the circle size by that method, there is a lower limit of 3.14 square inches and an upper limit of 12.56 square inches (assuming pi is equal to 3.14). The average of these two values—the midpoint value—is not 7.065 square inches, as would be the case for a diameter of 3 inches. Instead, it is (3.14 + 12.56)/2 = 7.85 square inches, which corresponds to a diameter of about 3.16 inches. Unless you specify which method to use to determine the size of the circle, the answer cannot be obtained.

It is important to always remember that probabilities are based on the results of many trials in actual practice. There is just one circle in the above-mentioned situation; it is either smaller in diameter than 3 inches or 3.16 inches, or it is larger. There actually is no probability involved unless you get, say, a thousand people to draw circles on pieces of paper according to these instructions and tally up the results.

## Sum of Irrationals

Can you find two irrational numbers that, when summed, yield a rational number? An integer?

At first, this might sound like an impossible problem to solve. Any irrational number, when written in decimal form, has a string of digits that is nonrepeating and nonterminating. For example, consider the value of pi = 3.14159 . . .. Is there any number that can be added to pi in order to get an integer, say 10? How would such an irrational number be calculated, and if found, how could it be proven that it really did add together with pi to form exactly 10?

One solution is to consider 10 as the nonterminating, repeating decimal value 9.99999 . . .. Subtracting pi from this gives

$$
\begin{array}{r}
9.99999 \ldots \\
- \ 3.14159 \ldots \\
\hline
6.85840 \ldots
\end{array}
$$

This difference is also irrational, because the digits of pi, subtracted always from the digit 9, are as unpredictable and nonterminating as the number pi itself. Thus there are indeed two irrational numbers that add up to exactly 10.

The whole question of irrationality is a strangely paradoxical one. How can the decimal expansion of pi really be nonterminating and nonrepeating? It can never be expanded all the way out, or at least no one yet has come to the last nonzero digit of its decimal expansion. How can such an expansion really exist anyway if the universe is such that the physical writing of the digits cannot be carried out within it? You can always find the next digit of pi using a computer. In this sense, the digits cannot be considered "random" because of the predictability of what the next one will be; in fact, it already exists and you only have to find it. But such thinking is the result of a finite mind trying to conceive an infinitely complicated quantity.

In fact, any irrational number can be added to some other irrational number to get any integer you desire. The same technique can be employed as was done with the above example.

There are many irrational numbers that can be multiplied by other irrationals resulting in a known rational number or integer. A very simple example is the product $\sqrt{2} \sqrt{8}$. Both of these numbers are irrational, but their product, $\sqrt{16}$, is the integer 4. Finding some irrational number that can be multiplied by *any* chosen irrational, however, is not always an easy thing to do. If fact you cannot even be certain it is always possible without engaging in proofs or investigations that are well beyond the scope of this book.

## Points on a Line

Perhaps you have heard that there are infinitely many points on any line segment of any length. This is true, or at least it is accepted by most people and by all mathematicians as true. In fact, the number of points on a line segment of unit length (finite length) is the same as the number of points on a ray starting at one point and proceeding infinitely far off in a single direction. How can this be proven?

Consider all of the real numbers such that $0 < x < 1$. This is an open interval, or line segment, on a number line (Fig. 1-7A). Also consider the set of reals such that $1 < x$. This takes the form of a ray on the number line, without the left-hand end point (Fig. 1-7B).

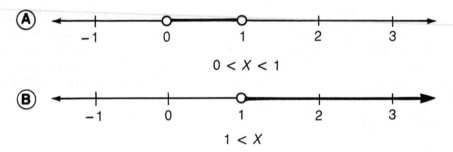

Fig. 1-7. At (A), open interval $0 < x < 1$. At (B), ray $1 < x$.

The number of points in the open line segment is equal to the number of points in the open-ended ray. This is easy to demonstrate. How can we say this? Both geometric objects contain an infinite number of points, so you could say that infinity is equal to itself and that the proof is therefore trivial. But it isn't quite that simple. There are different "types" of infinity, and they are not necessarily "equal."

Two sets are equal in size, or cardinality, if and only if the members of one set can be paired off in a one-to-one correspondence with the members of the other set. For each point $x_1$ such that $0 < x_1 < 1$, there is a corresponding point $x_1{}^*$ such that $1 < x_1{}^*$. We simply say that $x_1{}^* = 1/x_1$. Each point in the open interval $0 < x < 1$ has exactly one corresponding reciprocal in the open-ended ray $1 < x$. Therefore, the sets contain exactly equal numbers of points.

The number of points on a line segment or ray is *not* the same as the infinity of the integers, however. The integers are said to be *countably* infinite, and the cardinality of the set of integers is defined as *aleph nought*. Georg Cantor is credited with having shown that the cardinality of the set of integers is not equal to the cardinality of the set of real numbers. That cardinal number is called *aleph one* and is in a certain sense "greater" than *aleph nought*, because an attempt to pair off the set of integers with the set of real numbers does not result in a one-to-one correspondence. There are too many real numbers. For a more thorough discussion of this, a book on set theory is recommended.

## The Wheel Paradox

A famous paradox that is not very widely publicized but is capable of causing much consternation among those who cannot see the explanation concerns a pair of concentric wheels. Both are rigidly attached to each other so that one rotation of the large wheel is attended by exactly one rotation of the smaller wheel. An example is shown in Fig. 1-8. For example, you could glue a dime onto the center of a silver dollar to obtain this double wheel.

Imagine that this wheel rolls along a double surface, as shown in the diagram, so that the large wheel makes exactly one rotation along the lower surface. If the diameter of the larger wheel is $d_L$, then the length of the path along the surface for one rotation is approximately $3.14d_L$, where 3.14 is an approximation of the circle constant pi ($\pi$).

The upper surface is spaced just right so that the smaller wheel can roll along it while the larger wheel rolls along the lower surface. The smaller wheel has a diameter of $d_s$, where again $d_s < d_L$. The smaller wheel rolls at exactly the same revolution rate as the larger wheel because the two are rigidly attached to each other. Therefore, when the larger wheel rolls once, so does the smaller wheel—but it traverses the same distance ($3.14d_L$) as the larger wheel. How is this possible? It ought to only go a distance of $3.14d_s$. Since $d_s < d_L$, then $3.14d_s$ cannot possibly equal $3.14d_L$, yet this is apparently the case.

The catch is that the smaller wheel must slide along the upper surface if the larger wheel rolls along its surface. The points on the smaller wheel do, however, line themselves up in a one-to-one fashion with the points on the upper surface, despite the sliding—and it is this fact that confuses people who get fooled by this paradox.

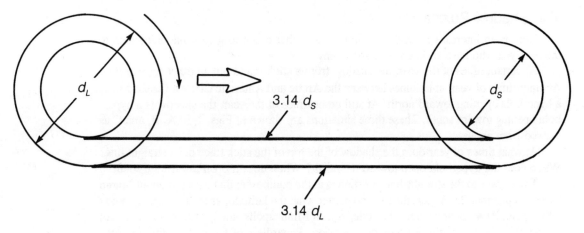

Fig. 1-8. The wheel paradox.

Another way of looking at this paradox is to consider two squares, instead of circular wheels, as shown in Fig. 1-9. The larger square bumps along its surface, without sliding either forward or backward. The smaller square is just the right size to fall flush with the upper surface when the squares are not up on a corner. As the larger square bumps along, the smaller square makes contact with its surface only when the larger square has one of its sides lying flat. Thus the smaller square traces a dotted line on the upper surface, while the larger square traces a continuous line on its surface.

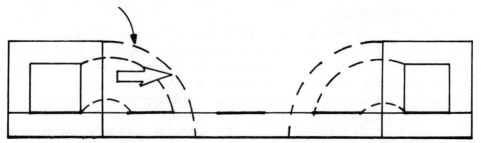

Fig. 1-9. The wheel paradox as illustrated using squares instead of circular wheels.

Imagine a regular pentagon, hexagon, septagon, octagon, and so on, one inside the other, instead of the square, and the result is always that the smaller figure will trace out a dotted line on the upper surface if the larger figure traces out a solid line on the lower surface. As the number of sides in the figure increases—that is, as the figure approaches a perfect circle—the dotted line gets finer and finer, with a limit being a "dust" of points that appears to be a solid line in a practical sense but is actually "dilute" in a mathematical sense. This is how Galileo Galilei observed the circle paradox, originally conjured up, according to legend at least, by Aristotle. Therefore, imagine extending the number of sides of a polygon to "infinity." The smaller wheel indeed rolls along its surface without sliding but instead traces out a "dilute" set of points. In physical reality, the smaller wheel would slide, as you can verify for yourself by constructing an apparatus and carrying out the experiment.

## The Shadow Puzzle

Here is an interesting puzzle, or brain teaser, that ought to give some enjoyment to those of you who have an interest in astronomy.

At certain times of the year, the shadow from a stick traces out an exact straight line. At other times of year, at latitudes between the Arctic and Antarctic Circles, the shadow is a hyperbola opening toward north. At still other times of the year, the shadow is a hyperbola opening toward south. These three situations are shown in Figs. 1-10 A, B, and C as viewed from above.

At what times of year does the shadow of the top of the stick trace out a straight line? When does the hyperbola open toward the north? When does it open toward the south?

The answer to the straight-line question is at the equinoxes; that is, on or about March 21 and September 23. This is the case no matter what the latitude, as long as you are not at either pole. At 45 degrees north latitude, say, in Minneapolis, the length of the stick will be the same as the length of its shadow at noon. Regardless of the latitude the line runs east and west in this case.

Between March 22 and September 22, the hyperbola will open towards the south. The closer the date is to the summer solstice, the more the hyperbola will deviate from a straight line. The exact shape of the hyperbola depends on latitude. North of a certain latitude, depending on the date, the hyperbola closes off into an ellipse, and is actually a parabola at one particular latitude. Can you figure out the exact latitudes, or at least the general nature of the problem?

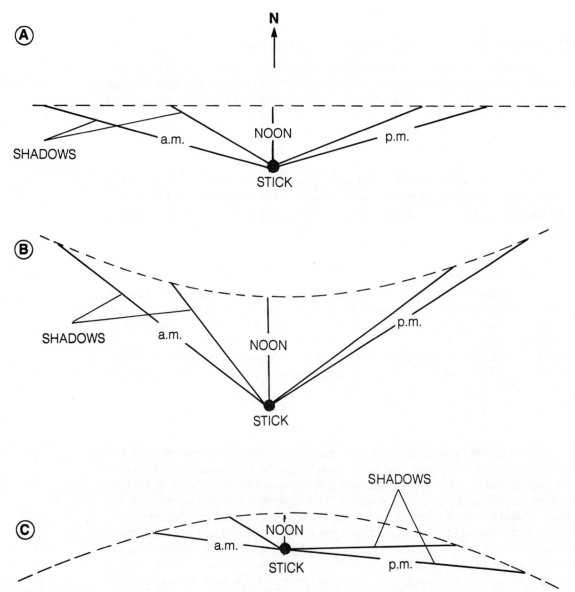

**Fig. 1-10.** Shadows cast by a stick, top view. At (A), a straight line is traced out by the tip of the stick throughout the day; at (B), the tip of the stick traces a hyperbola opening northward; at (C), it traces a hyperbola opening southward. These illustrations are for the Northern Hemisphere. North is toward the top in each illustration.

Between about September 24 and March 20, the hyperbola will open toward north. If the latitude is sufficiently far south, the shadow of the stick will trace out a parabola, and if it is still farther south, an ellipse. At a certain northerly latitude, the shadow disappears altogether—that part of the world where the sun is below the horizon continuously for all or part of that period.

The problem has many combinatorial particulars that can make good conversational brain teasers. For example, you could ask, "At what part or parts of the world does the tip of the shadow of a stick trace out a parabola?"

## Diagonals of Squares, Cubes, and Hypercubes

The length of the diagonal of a square measuring one unit on a side is $\sqrt{2}$ units. This is not difficult to prove by using the familiar Pythagorean theorem for right triangles (Fig. 1-11A). If the diagonal ($d$) is the hypotenuse, and if the base and height of a right triangle both equal one unit,

$$1^2 + 1^2 = d^2$$
$$d = \sqrt{1^2 + 1^2} = \sqrt{2}$$

How do you determine the length of the diagonal of a cube? One way is to consider the base of a right triangle as the diagonal of the square that forms the base of the cube; a unit-length edge of the cube is the height (Fig. 1-11B). Then if $d$ is the diagonal of the unit cube,

$$1^2 + \sqrt{2}^2 = d^2$$
$$d = \sqrt{3}$$

The four-dimensional cube, also called a *tesseract*, is impossible to fully diagram, although projections of it can be illustrated in three dimensions. A unit tesseract measures one unit on each edge and has cubic faces; each cube face has a diagonal measuring $\sqrt{3}$ unit because each face is a unit cube, just like any unit cube in three dimensions. Without even being able to visualize it, we can prove that the diagonal of a unit tesseract must therefore be $\sqrt{4}$ unit, of 2 units. Construct a right triangle with base $\sqrt{3}$ unit and height one unit. Then the diagonal, $d$, is found by

$$1^2 + \sqrt{3}^2 = d^2$$
$$d = \sqrt{4} = 2$$

One method of "visualizing" a tesseract in the meter-kilogram-second (MKS) system is to envision a cube measuring one meter on each edge that lasts for exactly one second. Another method would be to imagine a cube that measures 186,282 miles (299,792 kilometers) on an edge and lasts for one second. That distance is one light-second—the distance traveled by light in a second—and is therefore a sort of absolute equivalent in spatial terms of one second in time. Right angles between the time line and the three spatial dimensions are a little bit of a stretch of the imagination, but such a feat of daydreaming is not impossible. (There are people who claim to have trained themselves, after years of practice, to envision four spatial dimensions, but I am inclined to think that they are most likely just exhibiting symptoms of a tired brain if that is the case.)

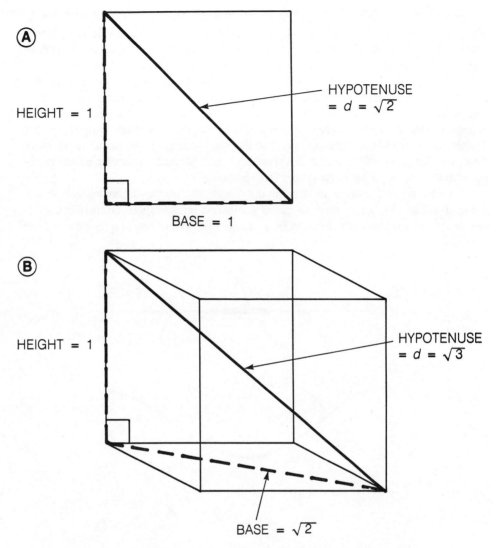

**Fig. 1-11.** At (A), diagonal of a unit square. At (B), diagonal of a unit cube.

It is not especially difficult to prove that the diagonal of a unit-$n$ cube is always equal to $\sqrt{n}$, where $n$ is the number of dimensions and is an integer greater than or equal to 2. You might already have done this in a mathematics class in high school or college. The principle of mathematical induction is the key. I leave a formal proof up to you.

## Are There Really Four Dimensions?

For mathematicians, the question of whether there could actually be more than three spatial dimensions, in the physical universe, is not important. Mathematically, there can be any integral number of dimensions (and even fractional numbers of dimensions according to certain definitions). The first hint that a spatial fourth dimension might really exist was provided not by mathematicians, but by astronomers. They have noticed, with the aid of Einstein's general theory of relativity, that space appears to be non-Euclidean rather than strictly Euclidean. The familiar postulates of Euclid do not apply in a non-Euclidean plane or space; hence the origin of this term for defining "curved" continuums.

Gravitational fields, as well as acceleration, tend to create the "curvature of space" that results in the breakdown of the postulates of Euclid. If three-space is actually non-Euclidean, this implies the existence of a fourth spatial dimension in which the curvature is possible. Most cannot readily visualize a four-space; this would involve placing four straight sticks together at a common point so that each stick is perpendicular to the other three, and this is not within our limited power to "see." Mathematicians have been working with such concepts for many generations, however.

The way in which space is distorted in the vicinity of a source of gravitation is shown in Fig. 1-12. At (A), a very weak source of gravitation renders space essentially Euclidean, or "flat," depicted in the drawing by a straight line (reduced by two dimensions). At

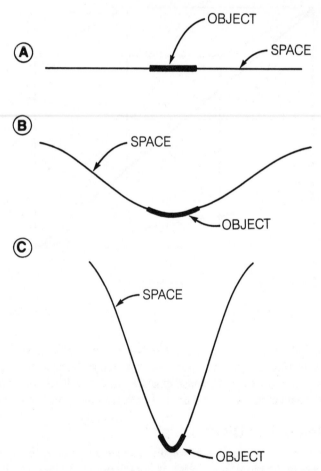

**Fig. 1-12.** Effect of gravitation on space. At (A), the effect is not discernible. At (B), space is "curved" significantly; at (C), greatly. These drawings are dimensionally reduced so that three-space appears as a line.

(B), a stronger source of gravitation bends space; that is, distance appears to increase radially in the vicinity of the object. If the source of gravitation is extreme, which is believed to be the case with collapsed stars, the distortion could be such that distances are tremendously increased, as shown at (C). The ultimate situation is the severance of the object from space as we know it. The gravitation becomes such that even light cannot escape the object.

How could this theory be tested to see whether in fact a curvature does occur in three-space in the vicinity of a source of gravitation? One way is to check the light from distant stars and see if the light rays are bent when the source of gravitation passes close to the stars in the sky. The effect of light-beam bending would cause stars to appear displaced outward from their normal positions when the source of gravitation passed near them. The most convenient source of intense gravitation available to us is the sun; measurements have actually been made using sensitive apparatus, and the curvature of space is indeed present—or at least the bending of light occurs exactly according to the theory of curved space.

Some astronomers and cosmologists theorize that there could be spaces having as many as 11 dimensions. There are problems with spaces of less than, or more than, three dimensions, however. The alimentary canal of a two-dimensional creature, for example, would cut the creature in half. In four dimensions, gravitation would obey an inverse-cube law rather than the inverse-square law as in three dimensions; this would render planetary orbits very improbable because only certain very special cases would result in the planets not falling into the sun or flying off into interstellar space. In five or more dimensions, these problems would be compounded even more. This is discussed in Stephen Hawking's book, *A Brief History of Time.* * Hawking also gets into some discussion of what he thinks has happened to universes of more than three dimensions.

## Time Travel

The advent of relativity theory has posed the very real possibility of traveling into the future. The scenario is well known: a space traveler accelerates to a very large fraction of the speed of light, say $0.999c$ (where $c$ is the speed of light) and maintains this speed for a great distance. In one example, the traveler takes off for Proxima Centauri, the nearest star (other than our own sun) which is about $4^1/_3$ light years distant. He returns about 8 years and 8 months later by Earth time, having aged only a day. If this traveler had an older sister, say 4 years older than himself, and went on this journey, he would return to find the woman almost 13 years older than himself. She could go instead and come back finding her younger brother now her older brother. In other examples, a space traveler goes off to the Andromeda galaxy, about $2.2 \times 10^6$ light years away, and returns to find—what?

Time travel into the future is entirely possible and does not lead to any paradoxes at all, provided you have a good understanding of relativity theory. Traveling into the future is equivalent to removing a piece of the time line from the present and immediate future, and repositioning it in the more distant future (Fig. 1-13). This causes a stretching of time in the relative sense from one viewpoint as compared with another; but it does not create any contradictions. Backward time travel is a different situation.

---

*Stephen W. Hawking, *A Brief History of Time* (New York: Bantam Books, 1988): 162-65.

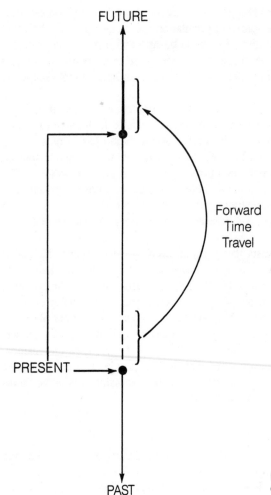

FUTURE

Forward
Time
Travel

PRESENT

PAST

**Fig. 1-13.** Illustration on the time line of travel into the future.

If it were possible to travel into the past, say a year ago, it would be possible to rewrite history. For example, one might prevent the time machine from ever being made operational, thereby preventing the very trip that allowed such sabotage. An infinite variety of other contradictions can be found. Traveling backward in time is equivalent to removing a piece of the time line from the present and the immediate future, and repositioning it in the past, over a part of the time line through which the "point of the present" has already passed (Fig. 1-14). Once this contradiction is made possible, the moon might as well be made of green cheese.

This argument is generally taken as proof that backward time travel isn't possible. Yet, physicists believe there may be real particles for which time is in fact reversed, just as there are antimatter particles such as positrons and anti-protons. The particles in question—at least one type of such particles—are *tachyons*, supposedly moving at speeds greater than the speed of light.

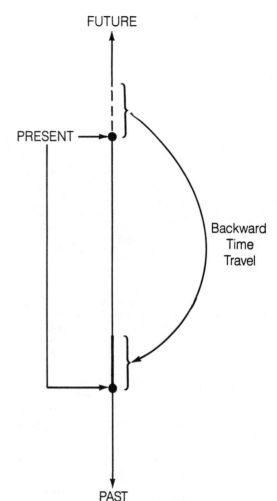

FUTURE

PRESENT ——

**Fig. 1-14.** Illustration on the time line of travel into the past.

Backward
Time
Travel

PAST

All of this, and all of recent physics, makes it clear that finding the absolute truth in our cosmos is probably just about as difficult as finding the exact value of pi by writing out its decimal expansion in full. These ideas might develop more and more "accurate" models of reality, but in the true sense of mathematical perfection, a full understanding of it might never be achieved.

Yet pi can be easily constructed geometrically by drawing a circle around its diameter. Draw a straight line with an unmarked straightedge, place the center point of a compass on the line, draw a circle of arbitrary size, and the ratio is right there before you, easily visible—and, from a decimal standpoint, completely out of reach.

Hawking has expressed wonder at how we seem not to be able to accept that the universe can "just be." We appear concerned about its evolution and fate to such an extent that we may be overlooking the obvious. It is a true paradox that the search for truth can lead us into such complications that we overlook simplicity itself.

And now, it's time for me to get back to work on that time machine.

# CHAPTER 2

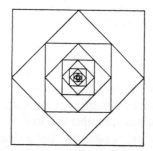

# Famous Problems and Puzzles

CERTAIN MATHEMATICAL PROBLEMS HAVE CONFOUNDED SCIENTISTS AND MATHEMA-ticians, as well as mapmakers and other scientists, for thousands of years. Some of the most well-known of these problems involve simple geometric constructions. Others are in the realm of number theory, a field that still allows exploration by students as young as junior and senior high-school age. Other problems are more sophisticated in their nature, involving statistical analysis and illusions. This chapter depicts some of these famous problems and puzzles.

## Trisecting an Angle

Geometric construction makes use of a compass and an unmarked straightedge to create various figures such as equilateral triangles, squares, line segments bisected and *n*-sected (where *n* is any integer). It is possible to perform quite sophisticated geometric feats with these simple tools, along with a fine pencil or marking pen. The compass can draw circles ideally of any diameter as small or as large as the pencil or pen point and paper size make practical. It is only necessary to know the center point of the circle and, in certain cases, the radius. The straightedge allows construction of Euclidean "straight" line segments of any length, from the smallest that is distinguishable from a mere point to the longest that the paper will allow. In some cases, one point on the line is known; in other cases, two are known.

Certain acts in construction are considered "cheating." These acts are, in general, any that involve doubt or imprecision or any form of guessing. Marking the straightedge is out. This includes marking it by holding the compass on it or against it.

Certain angles can be trisected without too much difficulty. An example of an angle that is quite easy to trisect is the 90-degree (right) angle. Actually this can be done by constructing a fixed 30-degree angle along the same base. The sine of 30 degrees is 0.5;

therefore, constructing a 30-degree right triangle is easy enough. I leave it up to you to figure this out; another method of trisecting the 90-degree angle is shown in Fig. 2-1.

Bisecting the 30-degree angle gives an angle of 15 degrees, and this is exactly $1/3$ of a 45-degree angle. Bisecting any angle is next to trivial. Therefore, once the 90-degree angle is trisected, the trisections are of any fraction $1/2^n$ of this angle, where $n$ is a positive integer.

You cannot construct an angle of any arbitrary number of degrees. Some special cases are possible such as $90/2^n$, $30/2^n$, or in a paradoxical way, any randomly constructed angle divided by $2^n$ where $n$ is a positive integer. But when randomly constructing an angle, it's guaranteed it measures an irrational number of degrees. This is because there are infinitely more irrationals than rationals; another way to say this is that the set of irrationals is infinitely more dense than the set of rationals. But a detailed discussion of that belongs under another heading in some other chapter or some other book. In other words, you cannot construct an angle of a given number of degrees, say 1.5787 degrees, using the traditional compass and straightedge. Perhaps when you were in school, you worked at this problem and came up with a method that appeared to work. I recall spending time at this at the blackboard before or after class. There was a blackboard-size compass and an unmarked length of wooden stripping, and I found a method that seemed to divide any given angle into thirds.

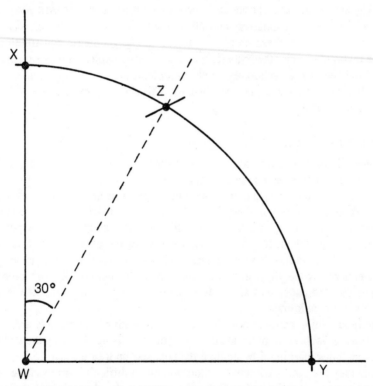

**Fig. 2-1.** Trisecting a 90-degree angle ⊿XWY is accomplished by leaving the compass set for the circle radius WX or WY, placing the center of the compass at point Y, and locating the intersection point Z (as described in the text).

"He did it," one of the girls said. (My mathematics skill was respected, at least, by the females; I wasn't known for beating up my classmates physically, so I did it mathematically.)

It looked as if she was right. But according to P. L. Wantzel, the mathematician of the nineteenth century, she was wrong. This French mathematician published the first rigorous proof that a general trisection is not possible via conventional geometric construction process.

A simple, crude attempt at trisection is shown in Fig. 2-2. Simply draw a line segment connecting two points equidistant from the vertex of the angle, and trisect the line segment. (The trisection of the line segment is not shown in the figure.) Then, drawing lines from the vertex through the trisection points gives an approximate trisection of the angle. Note that this will only work for angles less than 180 degrees. It is never a perfect trisection, although for very small angles, it is *almost* a perfect trisection. But in mathematics, "almost" is no better than "nowhere near."

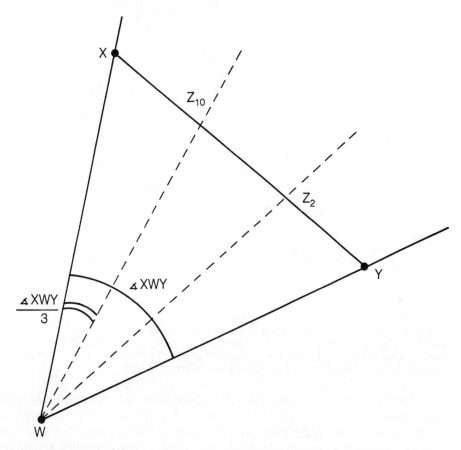

**Fig. 2-2.** Approximate method of trisecting an angle. Lengths WX and WY are equal. Trisect the line segment XY, which gives points $Z_1$ and $Z_2$. The angles $\angle XWZ_1$, $\angle Z_1WZ_2$ and $\angle Z_2WY$ are then approximately one-third the measure of $\angle XWY$.

Another approach is to divide the angle in half—bisect it—and then draw a line connecting equidistant points from the vertex of the half angle. Trisect this line segment and draw a line from the vertex through the appropriate trisection point. This comes very close to trisecting the original angle (Fig. 2-3). The error will in fact be so small that it is less than the error caused by imperfections in the drawing apparatus. However, this is still only an approximate trisection of the angle.

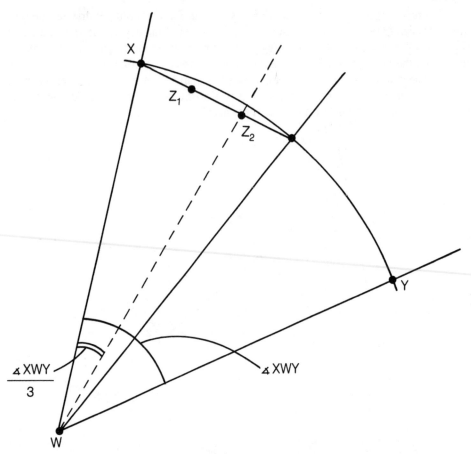

**Fig. 2-3.** A more accurate, but still approximate, method of trisecting an angle ∡XWY. First bisect the angle. Then draw a circle of radius WX = WY. Then use the point where this circle intersects the angle bisector as the end point of a line segment with X, and trisect this line segment to obtain points $Z_1$ and $Z_2$. The angle ∡XWZ$_2$ is then approximately one-third the measure of ∡XWY.

There is a way to trisect an angle by breaking one of the constraints normally applied to construction process. This method is shown in Fig. 2-4. First draw a straight line through the vertex point of the angle (an angle less than 180 degrees). Then draw a half circle with its center at the vertex point and pass it twice through the line segment and cross each of the rays that depict the angle. Extend the line segment in one direction, say toward the right, for a great enough distance to facilitate the rest of this process. Keep the compass at the radius value of the semicircle. Hold the straightedge so that it passes

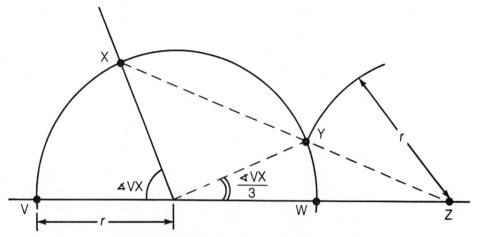

**Fig. 2-4.** A cheating method of exact angle trisection.

through point X. Hold the compass against the straightedge as shown. Then, manipulate the straightedge so that its axis and marker tip touch some point Y, as shown, and draw the line segment through the vertex of the angle at some point Z outside the half circle. The angle denoted by the arc YW is exactly one-third the size of the angle denoted by the arc VX.

This method constitutes cheating because the straightedge and the compass are manipulated together, "zeroing in" on certain points by visual estimation or guessing. In a rigorous construction, although there is always a certain inaccuracy because the apparatus is not precise, there is never any guesswork. The location of points Y and Z in Fig. 2-4 is a guessing game. You are, in effect, picking or locating specific points from an infinitude of choices in their vicinity. This can be done only to within the limits of the error introduced by the thickness of the lines and our ability to perceive exact points on such lines.

There is another way of looking at the trisection process, a way that is interesting, but is not really a rigorous solution to the problem. When you observe an angle from some point outside the plane on which it is drawn, its apparent measure depends on the angle that the observer looks down on it. To illustrate this, a right angle appears to measure 90 degrees only when it is observed from a point such that a line drawn from the observing eye to the vertex of the angle is 90 degrees (Fig. 2-5A). If you look down from some point that is "over" a point in the plane such as in Fig. 2-5B, the right angle appears obtuse. If you move so that your eye is over a point as illustrated in Fig. 2-5C, the angle appears acute. In fact, a 90-degree angle can be made to appear to measure any value $x$, such that $0 < x < 180$ (degrees), if the observation point P is properly located outside the plane in which the angle is contained.

Since trisecting a 90-degree angle is one of those specialized cases that is possible via rigorous geometric construction process, you can trisect any angle greater than zero degrees and less than 180 degrees simply by looking at the trisected right angle from the proper point of view. For example, from the viewpoint of Fig. 2-5B where the large angle appears to be 150 degrees, the trisected right angle seems to be broken into three 50-degree parts. Similarly at Fig. 2-5C, if the right angle looks like it measures just 45 degrees, it will appear to be trisected into 15-degree parts.

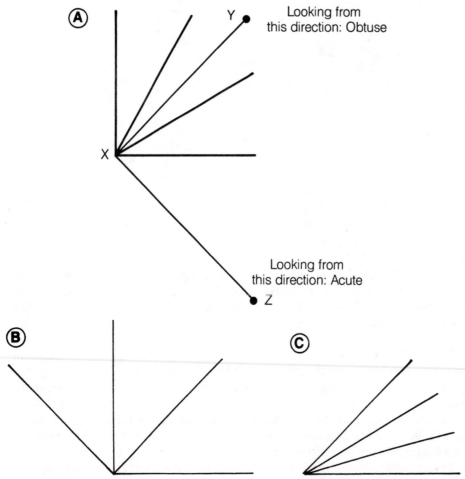

Fig. 2-5. Perspective method of angle trisection. Begin with a 90-degree angle that has been trisected by known means (A). Viewed from points in the direction XY, the angle appears obtuse (B); viewed from points in the direction XZ, it appears acute (C). The exact perspective can yield an angle having any measure greater than 0 and less than 180 degrees.

The fact remains, however, that when using a compass and unmarked straightedge in two dimensions, angle trisection has been proven impossible in the general case. The perspective in the drawings at Figs. 2-5B and 2-5C would render the circles, drawn by the compass, distorted into ellipses. This is why you cannot "project" a construction from one point of view to another in this general way.

Other tricks for angle trisection abound. If a watch or clock is allowed to run so that the minute hand spans an angle four times the measure of the given angle, the hour hand will move in the same length of time over an angle that is $1/3$ the measure of the given angle. Similarly, if the second hand of a clock is allowed to go 20 times the measure of a certain angle, the minute hand will go $1/3$ the measure of the angle. These are not constructions but they are interesting illustrations. The trick lies in using a clock in which the hands move continuously. Most modern quartz watches do not work this way; the hands move in little increments. An electric clock would work, but getting the exact point in time would be impossible because such a point lasts for an infinitesimal period and by the time you realize the hands are in the correct positions, they have gone past them. (Well, it was a good idea while it lasted—but that was no time at all.)

It is fascinating that some amateur mathematicians continue to search for rigorous ways to trisect angles in general by compass and unmarked straightedge. They do this despite being able to fully comprehend each step of the proof that trisection, in general, cannot be done. This proof, not explained in detail here, can be found in geometry text-books. One method consists of demonstrating that, if you assume that a 60-degree angle can be trisected, there is a contradiction; therefore, since the 60-degree angle cannot be trisected, trisection in general is not possible.

## Euclid's Parallel Postulate

A familiar, seemingly intuitive postulate in Euclidean geometry is as follows: Given a line L and a point P not on the line, there exists exactly one line L* through this point P that is parallel to the original line. The postulate might be illustrated as shown in Fig. 2-6.

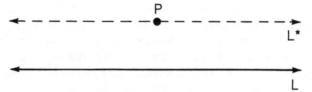

Fig. 2-6. The Parallel Postulate states that for a given line L and a point P not on L, there exists exactly one line L* through P that is parallel with L. This postulate has been found to be undecidable. Accepting it results in Euclidean geometry; refuting it results in non-Euclidean, but still consistent, geometry.

There are, of course, an infinite number of lines that can pass through P without inter-secting the original line; these lines cannot, however, be in the same plane with the origi-nal line. Add the constraint that the line L* through the point P must be in the same plane as the original line, and you can then say that there exists one and only one line L* through P that does not intersect the original line; this line L* is the one parallel line with the original line.

This apparently obvious property of points, lines, and planes is not a simple thing at all when the postulate is modified as above. With the refined version, speaking of a plane, there could be no lines through a point that never intersect the original line. This is the case, for example, if the plane surface turns out to be the surface of a sphere. Be careful, however, to define the meaning of a "straight" line on the surface of a sphere, because there is no such thing in terms of the traditional definition. Call it a geodesic line, a great circle, or a straight line on a sphere. In this case, it is easy to see that there are no two different straight lines that are parallel. Try demonstrating this using a globe.

In our universe, if it is indeed a four-sphere with a three-space surface as some cos-mologists think, the same property would hold for "straight" lines. There would be no such things as "straight" lines. Even if "straight" was defined as "the path followed by a photon of radiant energy in a vacuum," there could be no such thing as a true, infinitely long, "straight" Euclidean line. If allowed to travel the whole circumference of the four-sphere, the photon would eventually come back to its starting point. According to modern cosmologists, this would be a distance of billions, or even hundreds of billions of light years; recent estimates of the circumference of the universe range from $2 \times 10^{10}$ to $2 \times 10^{11}$ light years. Nonetheless, in mathematical terms, such size is not infinite.

I recall imagining Euclidean points, lines, and planes when I was in high school. I saw points as, well, infinitely small dots. Lines were like infinitely thin, straight threads, going off without end in two opposite directions. Planes were infinitely expansive panes of frosted glass without the glass. These ideas cannot be true, even in a mathematical sense, in a universe that is finite yet unbounded. You might wonder, "Yes, but can't we imagine that such things are true? Can't we imagine Euclidean geometry to be valid? Is it not possible to accept the Parallel Postulate in our minds?" The answer is again a question: "Of what value is a concept that *cannot* be the case in the cosmos in which we live?" Euclid apparently never conceived of the idea that the universe might be the three-space surface of a four-sphere. It is not intuitively evident. You can't tell by strictly observing, at least not with today's equipment, that the entire cosmos is closed off on itself in some huge way that dwarfs even the "local group" of galaxies.

The ancients could not tell by simply gazing at the surface of the earth that they were standing on a gigantic quasi-sphere, either.

Actually, the Parallel Postulate was stated slightly differently by Euclid. It was the fifth of his ten original postulates and said that if a line L crosses two other lines M and N such that the sum of the interior angles on the same side of L is less than 180 degrees (a straight angle), then the two lines M and N must intersect on that side of L. This is shown by three examples in Fig. 2-7 A, B and C. It was the mathematician John Playfair, a Scotsman, who actually stated the fifth postulate in its "parallel" form.

Somehow, this postulate struck mathematicians at a soft spot in their brains. Attempts were made to prove the Parallel Postulate on the basis of Euclid's other postulates. It was a thorn in the sides of mathematicians for a long time; geometry would become simpler, more "elegant," if such a proof were found. It is always desirable to have the fewest possible number of axioms or postulates in a mathematical system. If there are too many postulates, the system either is "dirty" or, what is the worst possible thing, it is wrong—the postulates contain, somewhere in their logical consequences, a contradiction. A "perfect" mathematical theory is the sort of universe in which there are plenty of nontrivial results but no contradictions. It was probably thought by many that such a "perfect" theory would be of the sort that every statement could be proven either true or false, but this is generally not the case with mathematical universes. There are some statements that cannot be demonstrated either way. (This was proven by Kurt Godel much later, after most of classical mathematics had matured and seemed to have become overripe.) This fact, in itself, does not necessarily detract from mathematics; quite the contrary, it makes things more interesting. (The concept, "God exists!" could be put into this category of statements that cannot be proven one way or the other in the mathematical sense.)

Joseph Louis Lagrange, in the 1700s, believed he had proven the Parallel Postulate on the basis of the rest of Euclidean geometry. He believed that the proof that the interior angles of any triangle add up to 180 degrees was sufficient to prove the Parallel Postulate. But he abruptly changed his mind during a lecture.

A proof of the Parallel Postulate would seem to lend itself well to the technique of *reductio ad absurdum*, where it is assumed that there exist two lines through a given point not on a line and parallel to the original line. (It would seem obvious that there ought to be at least one.)

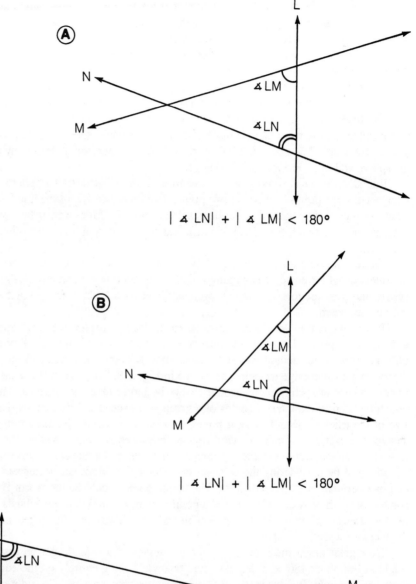

$$| \measuredangle LN | + | \measuredangle LM | < 180°$$

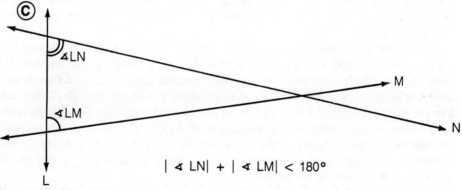

**Fig. 2-7.** Illustrations of various examples showing Euclid's Fifth Postulate. The drawings at (A), (B), and (C) show lines L, M, and N, with angles ∡LM and ∡LN. Angle measure is denoted by vertical lines (|∡LM| and |∡LN|).

However, it was eventually determined that the Parallel Postulate falls into that category of statements in Euclidean geometry that has no truth value either way; that is, it is one of the "bugs" that Kurt Godel proved must exist. We can get along without this postulate in geometry to some extent; however, the art is made truly "Euclidean" by including the Parallel Postulate as an axiom.

However, consider that through a given point not on a line, there exist *no* parallel lines. This is quite valid on the surface of a sphere, as can easily be verified using a globe. Any two lines that are geodesics and "locally straight" must intersect at exactly two points on the sphere, these two points being exactly opposite each other. (Consider two meridians and the North Pole and South Pole of the earth.) The interior angles of any triangle on the sphere add up to *more* than 180 degrees.

Euclid's original fifth postulate is also invalid on the surface of a sphere. Two lines intersect at some point—actually at two points, one on either side of the line L—no matter what the sum of the angles that the lines subtend with L. Moreover, if the two lines are straight, they must both cross L, at two different points, straight lines on a sphere all being geodesics.

There is no such thing as an infinitely long line on the surface of a sphere. However, the lines do not have end or beginning points. You can travel along any straight line on a sphere and continue forever, but will eventually get back to the starting point and trace it out all over again.

If we were two-dimensional beings on the surface of a sphere, and we knew that our universe was spherical but did not know how big it was, how could we tell how large our universe was? One method would be to employ straight-line-making devices, such as lasers, to construct large triangles, as shown in Fig. 2-8. The sum of the measures of the interior angles of such triangles would always be larger than 180 degrees. The extent to which the sum of the interior angles of a given size exceeded 180 degrees, based on the size of the triangle, would make it possible for us to calculate the circumference of the sphere. For example, if an equilateral triangle has three 90-degree angles, the side of the triangle is one-quarter of the circumference of the sphere. On the earth, this might be easily observed by considering the equator, the Greenwich Meridian (0 degrees longitude) and the meridian of 90 degrees west. The vertex points would be the North Pole, a point somewhat south of Accra, Ghana, and a point very near the Galapagos Islands. Each side of this triangle is approximately 6,200 miles long. Each interior angle measures 90 degrees, for a total of 270 degrees.

How great might the sum of the interior angles of a triangle get on a sphere? You might at first think 180 × 3 degrees, the "triangle" being entirely on the equator of the earth, for example. But this is still not the largest possible measure. Consider a triangle so large that its interior angles become the exterior angles of a smaller triangle. This smaller triangle might get so small that it has interior angles of total measure 180 degrees (essentially a plane triangle, being on such a small part of the sphere). The actual triangle under consideration would be the one whose interior angles were the exterior angles of the small triangle, each measuring, say, 300 degrees (if the triangle is equilateral) so that the total internal measure would be 900 degrees.

The triangle would then vanish to a point if it were made any larger, and repeating the process would be somewhat meaningless, like beginning the next cycle of a perfect sine

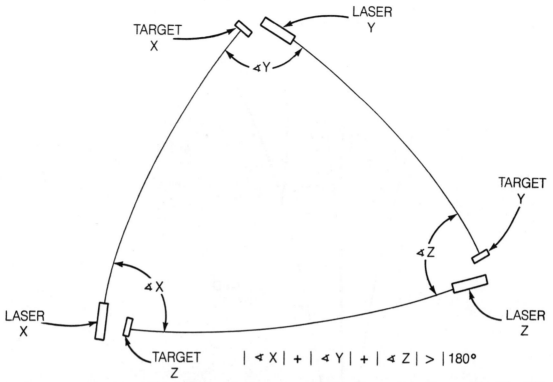

$$| \sphericalangle X | + | \sphericalangle Y | + | \sphericalangle Z | > | 180° $$

**Fig. 2-8.** Laser experiment for showing the total interior angle measure of a triangle on a sphere. The sum |X| + |Y| + |Z| is greater than 180 degrees and can be any value up to, but not including, 900 degrees.

wave. Thus on a sphere, a triangle can have interior angles the sum of which is anything greater than 180 degrees but less than 900 degrees.

Our universe is thought to be a gigantic four-sphere with a three-space surface in the generality, although locally, the situation is different. In the vicinity of a gravitational source such as the sun or the earth, space is supposedly curved into a funnel shape. A dimensionally reduced drawing of this is depicted in Fig. 2-9. The curvature is not nearly as great for the sun as is the case in Fig. 2-9; however, triangles in this kind of space may have measures totaling less than 180 degrees or more, depending on how they are oriented relative to the gravitational source. In general, if the source is inside the triangle, the total interior-angle measure will exceed 180 degrees; if the source is outside the triangle, the total measure of the interior angles will be less than 180 degrees. There are special cases in which the sum of the measures of the interior angles of a triangle is exactly 180 degrees.

If the whole universe is a four-sphere with a three-space surface, how can we be certain that distant galaxies are not actually closer? We might be looking all the way around the sphere, or more than halfway, and possibly several times around. It is doubtful that we would see repeats of galaxies behind each other, because the nearer image would get in the way. If galactic motion made it possible for us to see the galaxy twice or more, we would not recognize it as the same galaxy anyway, because, in the time required for light to make the extra circumnavigation of the universe, the appearance of the galaxy would have changed.

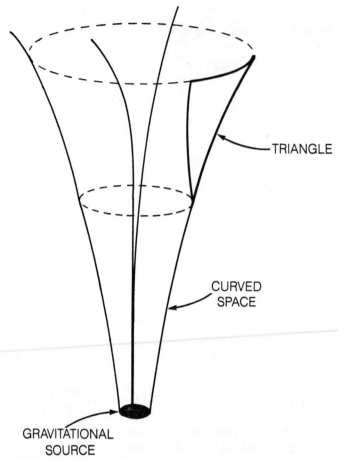

Fig. 2-9. Example of negatively curved space in which the sum of the measures of the interior angles of a triangle can be less than 180 degrees or greater, depending on the placement of the triangle.

We do not at present have access to distances great enough to conduct laser-triangle experiments to determine the size of the universe. However, estimates of its circumference range from $2 \times 10^{10}$ to $2 \times 10^{11}$ light years based on other observed characteristics of matter distribution in space.

Because there are infinitely many ways that a universe might be non-Euclidean, and only one way for a universe to be Euclidean, strict Euclidean geometry should get much less importance than it has received up to this day. The teaching of Euclidean geometry is useful for learning the technique of rigorous mathematical proof at the high-school level, but realize that in the "real universe," there actually are no Euclidean spaces. All dimensional spaces, at least up to four-dimensional space-time, are non-Euclidean, or "curved."

## Fermat's Last Theorem

The mathematician Pierre de Fermat of the 1600s was an amateur number theorist. Number theory is a discipline in mathematics that allows even high-school-level students to conduct original research, even today. Computers have not made it significantly easier to perform mathematical proofs of a rigorous nature in number theory. (In fact, the rigorous proof in all of mathematics still requires, most of the time, human insight not yet programmed into computers.)

Fermat always seemed to have a valid proof when he said he had one. But there is one frustrating instance in the history of mathematics where Fermat wrote in a margin something to the effect that "I've found a proof, but there isn't space enough here to write it out." Then he died before he got a chance to formally record his proof.

This proof was in regards to the Diophantine equation

$$x^n + y^n = a^n$$

Fermat thought he had proved that this equation could not be solved for integers $n$ where $n > 2$. No one has yet succeeded in proving this. I will, as other authors have, say that I don't want to see any such "proofs." I am not certain whether I would be qualified to evaluate them, and I don't have the time. Nonetheless, anyone who wants to try can go ahead; it has been a favorite pastime of people who like a mathematical challenge for over three centuries. It would seem that mathematical induction would be the way to go about proving this; that is, you could show that there is a solution for $n = 2$ (and indeed there is), and then you could show that if it holds for $n = c$, where $c$ is some integer, then it holds for $n = c + 1$, etc. The other possibility would be to assume that there can be no solutions for $n > 2$, and then derive a contradiction. That would require finding an actual solution, and a computer is the best tool to use in the search. That has been done for values of $n$ up to 125,000. If there is a counterexample, the numbers involved will have more than $10^6$ digits.

Certain subproofs have been realized concerning Fermat's Last Theorem, as this has been called. One such subproof is that it is true if it holds for all prime-number values of $n$ greater than 2. If this is the case—that the equation cannot be solved for any prime-number exponent greater than 2—then it cannot be solved for any exponent that is an integer and is greater than 2.

The theorem has been proven for $n = 3$, $n = 4$, $n = 5$ and $n = 7$. These proofs are not simple and they are not reproduced here. A book on Diophantine analysis is the source in which to look for such proofs if you are interested.

It has been theorized that this theorem may be one of those statements that Kurt Godel said must be undecidable. It can be proven, however, that if Fermat's Last Theorem is actually undecidable, it must be true—because if it were false, a single counterexample would exist disproving it! That seems to do away with that kind of "cop out."

Various mathematicians have attempted to prove Fermat's Last Theorem, and occasionally a "proof" has been found that appeared to be valid. On closer observation, however, every proof has been found to contain a flaw. Ferdinand Lindemann published a supposed proof of this theorem that was a long, involved discourse with its mistake at the very outset. Some mathematicians have steadfastly refused to attempt a proof, saying that it would most likely be a waste of time and an embarrassment in the end.

Colleges and universities generally return proofs submitted to them, saying they will not even look at them or they will examine them only for a fee. Thus, the omnipotent dollar rears its head even in the realm of pure mathematics. But why should busy scholars help out a fortune-seeker for no return at all?

## Statistical Objectivity

If you contemplate persistent mathematical problems, you will eventually come upon statistical "fudging." It simply cannot be avoided. The misuse, misrepresentation, or twisting of statistics is so habitual in our modern information-oriented society that no amount of watchfulness can completely protect against deception by this means.

One statistic that has gained a great amount of attention lately is the "national debt." Apparently the United States owes somebody a lot of money, and if the debt gets too large, something terrible will happen. But what? A general panic? Another Great Depression? The debt is referred to as constantly rising or as the rate of the rate of increase leveling off. And people are getting paid to talk about these things. The conservatives accuse the liberals of trying to scare people into accepting a tax increase to help "reduce the debt." (Without getting into opinions, that sounds like giving a chronic alcoholic a drink to keep him from getting the shakes, or a heroin addict some heroin to keep his belly from aching.)

Statistical analysis has been used to make scientific research seem legitimate. It lends a certain air of objectivity. But it can also trigger a warning signal: Beware of deception. It's all over the place.

Statistical analysis is nearly always, or always, subjective in some way. Somebody has to interpret the data. Experiments can be performed, but they always have to be done under controlled conditions. Some data is left out, and other data might be given exaggerated importance. I recall seeing a comparison graph in a diet book by Dr. John Yudkin. He was discussing the relationship between television sets purchased in England and the rate of heart attacks. The graphs paralleled one another so precisely that it seemed as if there must be some direct causal relationship between the two variables. But consider the following questions:

* What is the method of monitoring the occurrence of heart attacks?
* Does an increased sedentary lifestyle contribute?
* Do television sets produce some sort of dangerous radiation?
* Is the general increase in living standard with a richer diet part of the equation for both availability of television sets and heart disease?
* Does watching all those killings on television trigger some kind of unconscious stress factor?
* Does advertising of products on television lead to more consumption of goods that might contribute to heart disease?
* Does the advancement of technology make it easier to detect heart disease, concurrent with the invention of electronic devices such as television?
* Does the radio-frequency energy in all electronic devices, including television (which have all proliferated in roughly the same generation) cause heart disease?
* Does something in the spectrum of light from the picture tube trigger hormones that might increase heart disease?
* Is television and all the horrible things we see on television causing people to get more paranoid and only *think* they are having more heart disease?
* Is someone fudging the data?

This last question is not as silly as it sounds. An article in the February, 1989 issue of *Omni** contains some sobering information concerning possible scientific fraud. According to Walter Stewart, many mistakes in science are deliberate, are covered up, or both. So how can we believe that the graphs depicting the relationship between television sets sold and heart disease are valid at all? How do we know they haven't just been made up?

We don't. We're really gullible, and we've got to stop that if we want to know what's going on.

The above statements are bound to create a storm of protest. No one wants to be called a liar. Even if people are honestly trying to get at the truth, however, misinformation and misinterpretation of information still are abundant. There is no getting around this, so you have to be careful.

In the *American Scientist* for March and April, 1988, there is an article on precisely this subject: The illusory nature of the objectivity of statistics.* The data obtained for statistical analysis, the authors point out, is usually subjective, not objective. The intentions of the research person(s) tend to affect the outcome. For example, someone seeking to prove or support the notion that dietary cholesterol intake is a causative factor in atherosclerosis will tend to obtain data that supports this conclusion and neglect data that do not support it. This is not necessarily an intentional thing. In fact, it might be entirely subconscious. People want to see their own theories supported. This is evident throughout scientific history. Sometimes, scientists get such an emotional stake in their own particular set of beliefs that they directly attack (verbally) anyone who publishes material to the contrary. This calls attention away from the issue and toward the personal differences of the scientists. Thus, any real inquiry might be put off in favor of a discussion of a particular person's good or bad habits, or scientific thoroughness, or *Curriculum Vitae*.

Conflicts of interest are not at all unusual in this type of research bugaboo. For example, the sugar industry might fund research into the causative effects between sugar consumption and tooth decay; the tobacco industry might fund research into the causative relationship between smoking and emphysema, lung cancer, or heart disease. Nowadays, these relationships are accepted more or less as fact. However, this attitude is just as dangerous as the obvious conflicts of interest that occur in research funded by certain producers for research about their own products. For example, there is little objectivity in research study done by Russians concerning the threat of world communism. Why should people be any less cautious about research funded by producers of the materials involved? Often, though, these facts are covered up, deliberately or otherwise.

In America, money is a big deal. There's no getting around that. But the pursuit of money ought to have nothing to do with scientific research. Separating the two is not easy in practice. A system of checks and balances is necessary for every research project, especially those requiring large grants or those involving human life and safety.

Berger and Berry employ examples to differentiate between "standard" statistical analysis and "Bayesian" statistical analysis. They argue for the need to recognize the subjectivity of statistics. They use an example in which vitamin C is tested for effectiveness in

---

*Walter Stewart, "Interview," *Omni* (February 1989): 65.

*James O. Berger and Donald A. Berry, "Statistical Analysis and the Illusion of Objectivity," *American Scientist* (March/April 1988): 159–165.

reducing symptoms of the common cold. There are two possible hypotheses: Either vitamin C has an effect, or it has no effect. Actually there are three: vitamin C makes cold symptoms better; vitamin C has no effect; vitamin C makes cold symptoms worse. Most would not consider this last hypothesis at all, but it should be considered to be objective. If not, the approach of the whole experiment is biased, which could affect the "results."

You can approach this experiment as either having two possible conditions (vitamin C has an effect, or it does not), or three (vitamin C has a positive effect, a negative effect, or no effect). To be "objective," begin with the assumption that each case has equal "probability." Thus, for the two-case scenario, each would carry a "probability" of 50 percent; with three cases, each would have a "probability" of $33^{1}/_{3}$ percent. These percentages attach different "probabilities" to the outcomes. In the two-case scenario, the chance of vitamin C having a beneficial effect is 50 percent $\times$ 0.5 or 25 percent, but it is $33^{1}/_{3}$ percent in the three-case scenario. But remember, either it *is* beneficial or it *isn't*. It is a mistake to attach "probabilities" to phenomena that either take place or they do not. In a given person, vitamin C could actually have a physiological effect that is beneficial. In someone else, a placebo might work just as well, with the effect being entirely in the mind. In another type of person, a placebo or vitamin C may produce negative effects. (I recall reading a book that stated that certain types of viruses might turn into respiratory ailments if vitamin C were taken; such viruses require vitamin A instead.) Hence, the problem is extremely complex. Whether vitamin C works for you, does not work, or even makes you feel worse is something that you must determine. No one can say with absolute certainty that the "chances are such-and-such" that you will suffer less from a cold if you take vitamin C.

This is only one type of mistake that is made in statistical analysis—applying it when it really isn't appropriate. If you take samplings of people, you are actually determining the relative proportions of certain types of people, not the chances of vitamin C making your cold better! Another common type of error is more subtle, but it, too, involves a determination made before the experiment even begins. In their article, Berger and Berry explain this mathematically, based on the number of possible outcomes and their relative probabilities, along with the criterion for carrying the experiment further or stopping at a certain point.

If conclusive evidence is found for an effect after a given number of observations—say $n$—then the experiment is terminated. If the evidence is not conclusive after $n$ observations, then more observations are carried out, up to a predetermined number $x$. Most would not think that this way of doing the experiment would have any effect on the outcome, but it does. The two-stage plan is a form of contingency plan. Suppose it is not necessary to carry out $x$ observations, that conclusive evidence is found after only $n$ observations. The existence of the contingency plan doesn't seem to have any effect on the outcome. It hasn't even been used. But Berger and Berry demonstrate a way in which this contingency plan does affect the outcome. The exact details are sublime, and in order to understand the workings of the phenomenon, it is necessary to read the article. The point is that the method used in evaluating data determines, or has a significant effect on, the outcome of an experiment, even if the actual data is identical in every case.

As a final example, consider the probability that a particular hurricane will strike the Miami, Florida area. Suppose the hurricane is located in the Caribbean. You could consider every hurricane in the past 50 years that has been within 2 degrees of latitude and longitude of the given storm, and then find out how many of them—what proportion—proceeded to go on to produce hurricane-force winds (74 miles per hour or greater) within the boundaries of Dade County, Florida. This would be an extremely crude way of determining the "probability" that this storm would strike the area. The forecast could be improved by including details of the weather patterns over the continental United States, Atlantic Ocean, Caribbean Sea and Gulf of Mexico because these patterns influence the paths of hurricanes. These data could be compared with similar situations in the past 50 or even 75 years or as far back as knowledge of weather patterns and records go. This would result in a better idea of the chances of a hurricane-force storm striking in Dade County. But even with all of this data, a very accurate forecast is unobtainable until the storm is much closer to wherever it eventually does make landfall, if it does.

In the final analysis, the storm will either strike land or it will not. The winds will be a certain number of miles per hour at the maximum at a certain place if the storm makes landfall. It will only occur once. No other storm will ever be exactly like it, ever again, as long as there is an Earth on which hurricanes can form. Therefore, the whole business of estimating the probability that a hurricane will strike Miami is fabricated.

Even such a little event as a butterfly taking off in Tokyo in July might affect whether a hurricane strikes Miami in September. This is called the "Butterfly Effect" and is discussed in Chapter 5.

# CHAPTER 3

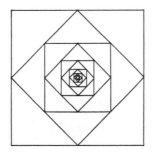

# The Search for Absolutes

Humans require some absolutes for peace of mind. Ever since communication has been possible between people, there have been expressions for absolute things. The planet Earth is a convenient absolute: for most of recorded history, it has been regarded as the center of the universe and the standard of reference on which all motion has been based. Later, astronomers deduced that the Earth revolves around the sun, and the sun was taken as the absolute reference point in the cosmos. Then, it was realized that the sun moves with respect to the other stars, which are themselves suns, some much larger and hotter than our own. The notion that any one of the stars (including our own sun) was absolutely fixed had to be discarded. Today we are almost convinced that there is no absolute standard of motion whatsoever. Almost, but not quite—there is still a certain longing for an absolute standard of motion in our minds, a persistent notion that such a thing *must* exist.

The same thing holds for time. Was there an actual beginning of time? Will time ever come to an end? We tend to think of time as a dimension, and often time is represented by a line along which we are presumed to be "moving"at a constant rate of "speed" (Fig. 3-1). When pressed to define the rate at which we move through time, the best answer is that we go a second per second, or a year per year—rather meaningless expressions of "speed." In the early part of this century, Albert Einstein found that this rate of movement through time was actually a relative thing based on point of view and might differ considerably from one particular viewpoint to another. Time could be dilated to any extent or any ratio such as 2 to 1, 5 to 1, 100 to 1, or even 1,000,000 to 1. In fact, Einstein showed it might be possible to have a billion years go by on the Earth, while we, in some fast-moving space ship, would perceive just a few months or years to pass. The well-known "twin paradox" arose from this proposition where two people might age at different rates, starting at the same age (identical twins, for example) and ending up a generation apart. Modern cosmologists have used all of Einstein's work, along with that of other scientists such

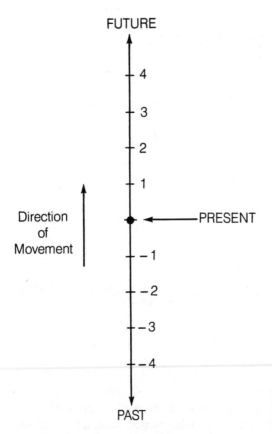

FUTURE

Direction
of
Movement

4

3

2

1

PRESENT

−1

−2

−3

−4

PAST

**Fig. 3-1.** The time line. Movement is at the rate of one unit per unit time toward the future. This is the standard depiction of time "flow."

as George Gamow, Sir Arthur Eddington, and Edwin Hubble to formulate a fantastic theory in which the universe is thought to have begun as a violent explosion some tens of billions of years ago. Prior to that—well, there is no prior to that, as far as the theory goes. *That* was the beginning of space and the beginning of time.

Some scientists find the idea of a creation more difficult to accept than the notion that things have always been and always will be. Thus, the so-called Big Bang theory has its counterpart in the Steady State theory. The proponents of these two theories have sometimes gotten into arguments where emotion seems to prevail over reason. One person likes the idea of creation, while another cannot accept finite time and space, and so each proceeds according to a belief based on personal preference. Either notion is difficult, however, to envision in its entirety. If there was a creation, how can we say that there simply was no time before that? If there was no creation, then where did everything come from? How can we simply say that it was always here? Yet, few would deny the statement that the truth must be either one way or the other—even if we can never know which.

## Absolute Position

Thinking of an absolute reference position often conjures the thought of a center for the universe. Depending on the geometry of the universe or the matter in the universe, such a point might exist and it might not. If it does exist, it might be in the universe or, oddly enough, it might not.

The most popular concept of the universe among lay people is that of an infinite expanse of stars and galaxies. No matter how far you go in any direction, according to this theory, there will be more and more stars and galaxies. In fact, this concept of the universe is almost certainly not a representation of the true case. If it were true, there could be no central point in the universe because of its infinite expanse. Any point would be just as good an absolute reference as any other point.

Another concept of the universe arises from the Big Bang theory. If all the matter in the whole cosmos were once at a single point or within a very small volume and there was subsequently an explosion that cast all the matter outward in all directions, then the universe must resemble a huge globular cluster of galaxies. The radius of the universe, in light years, would be determined by the initial speed of the exploded material and by the elapsed time since the explosion. If the fastest matter were thrust outward at the speed of light 20 billion ($2 \times 10^{10}$) years ago, then the radius of the universe must be $2 \times 10^{10}$ light years. The center (where the explosion began) would be roughly the average position of all the matter in the cosmos (Fig. 3-2).

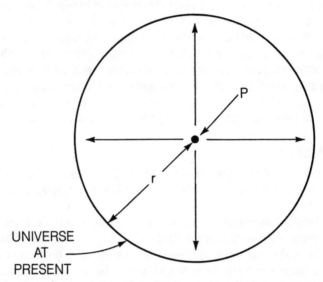

Fig. 3-2. The expanding universe, presumably beginning $r$ years ago, where $r$ is the radius in light years, and a big bang is assumed to occur at point P with outward velocity of the speed of light.

This notion of absolute position is dependent on the proposition that the explosion was symmetrical and also on the idea that space is Euclidean in its generality. Einstein showed that space is non-Euclidean, or, in a sense, curved, because of the effects of gravity. This result has been demonstrated experimentally by measuring, very precisely, the path taken by light rays as they pass near the sun from distant stars. The sun causes the stars nearly in line with it to appear to change position, compared to their positions when they are not anywhere near the sun in the sky. The light travels the shortest distance between two points, but this is not necessarily a straight line in a space that is not "flat." It has been suggested that the entire universe is non-Euclidean in its generality, in a way similar to the way the surface of the Earth is curved. If that is true, there may be an average position for all of the matter in the cosmos, but it might not lie within the cosmos as we know it, but in a place dimensionally removed. A good analogy, again, is if you think of the surface of Earth. The average position of all the points on the surface of a sphere is not, itself, a point on the surface of the sphere; rather, this point is at the center of the sphere.

In any case, the definition of the "average position"of all the matter in the universe is a horrendously difficult thing to put down. You could say that it is the average position, as calculated in three dimensions, of all the elementary particles in the whole of creation. We don't even know, for certain, what an elementary particle actually is or even if there is such a thing. If there are such things, they are all in extremely complicated motion, so much so that their positions can only be guessed at in terms of probabilities. It would be impossible to plug all of the coordinates of all of the elementary particles in the universe into a computer and have the result printed out. And even if this were somehow possible with a great computer that could perform the operation in a span of time less than a few human generations, then upon repeating the operation, the result would almost certainly be different, perhaps much different.

The most that can be said concerning the absolute standard of position is that we should choose a convenient reference point for the system in which we are operating. This might be New York City for the Earth, the sun for our solar system, and the center of the Milky Way for the galaxy. In fact, we have terrestrial coordinates (latitude and longitude), solar-system coordinates based on the plan of the ecliptic (the plane described by the orbit of our planet around the sun) and galactic coordinates (based on the plane defined by the disk of our spiral galaxy). Beyond that, we might someday have a use for a universe coordinate system, although it would be a great help for us to know the shape of the universe beforehand—and we haven't come to a complete agreement about that yet.

## Absolute Motion

Perhaps it is easier to define absolute motion than to attempt to establish absolute position. It is easy to tell if something is moving or if it is stationary, is it not? Of course, the answer is "no."

There are certain standards of motion that can immediately be discarded as impossible. One example is the surface of the Earth. A point on the surface of the Earth cannot be stationary in an absolute sense. If it were, the distant stars, revolving once around the Earth every 23 hours and 56 minutes, would have to be moving faster than the speed of light. As an example, Proxima Centauri, about 4.3 light years distant, would have to revolve around a path of 27 light years in circumference in just one day. That is almost 10,000 times the speed of light. This contradicts one of the most fundamental results of the special theory of relativity: that the speed of light cannot be attained, much less surpassed, by material objects. There would have to be a gravitational pull far greater than any force yet known in the universe between Proxima Centauri and the Earth to keep the star from flying away and disappearing altogether from view. All of the other stars, some much more distant, would also have to have this attraction for Earth, and the intensity of this force would have to increase with increasing distance, because of the increased speed of stars very far away as compared with those relatively nearby. A star on the opposite side of the galaxy, perhaps 70,000 light years distant, would revolve 440,000 light years in a single day, or 161,000,000 times the speed of light. Nonsense!

Using the Earth itself as a stationary object, presents the same problem on an even larger scale because of the movement of the sun with respect to the Earth. Pretend the sun completes one "orbit" around the Earth in 365-1/4 days. Then Proxima Centauri would go 27 light years in one year. That's not as fast as if we use a single point on the Earth for reference, but it's still impossible.

How about the sun? Can we consider it to be the absolute standard for motion in the universe? We have found, from observation using devices that measure Doppler shift at visible light wavelengths, that the sun is moving with respect to the other stars in our galaxy. We can consider the sun to be in relative motion as concerns these other stars. There is no special reason why we should consider the sun to be standing still while the other stars are all moving, although within the confines of our own galaxy, this does not appear to cause a contradiction with the principles of special relativity. The relative motions of all the stars within our galaxy are such that none of these other stars are moving at, or in excess of, the speed of light if the sun is the frame of reference. Consider that the sun rotates on its axis once in about four weeks; so it is the whole sun, not just one point on its surface, that must be thought of as the absolute frame of reference for motion.

It becomes difficult when going beyond our galaxy if the sun is used as the absolute motion standard. The entire Milky Way galaxy, a spiral some 100,000 light years in diameter ($6 \times 10^{17}$ miles), is rotating like a gigantic cosmic hurricane. The sun makes a course around the center of the galaxy along with all of the other stars so that the rest of the universe appears to go around and around, although slowly, if any single point in our galaxy is considered to be stationary. The problem is similar to what happens when the Earth is the absolute standard for motion, except the scale is many times larger. There is therefore no more justification in considering the sun as an absolute standard for motion than in considering such a reference to be Earth. It's an error to think of the entire universe rotating around and around *outside* our galaxy while our own galaxy does not rotate. Observation of other spiral galaxies indicates that they rotate; so ours must, too.

What if the galaxy represented a fixed frame of reference in the universe? The galaxy is just one of a "local group" of several separate galaxies, a cluster of galaxies, and these galaxies are all in motion with respect to each other. Therefore there is an even larger unit than the whole galaxy. Our local cluster of galaxies is the largest single unit that can be considered except for the entire universe itself. The universe must be stationary with respect to itself. The problem then lies in finding out which points are stationary relative to one point that is stationary relative to the whole universe. Once such a point is discovered, then all points with zero motion relative to that point are stationary in an absolute sense. How do you go about finding one such point?

Around the end of the nineteenth century, it was thought that light waves needed a medium in which to travel. Sound requires air or water or metal or some other material substance to be propagated; it was believed that light, having been found to have wavelike properties, needed some kind of medium. This medium was postulated to exist and was given the rather elegant name *luminiferous ether.* This ether had to be a strange kind of substance, because it permeated the vacuum of space and also could be passed through material substances such as water and glass, transparent to light. The ether also could pass through such substances as wood, which allows some electromagnetic fields to go through it. Iron and nickel, which do not pass electromagnetic fields, might thus be devoid of lumeniferous ether. But most of space had to contain it. Given the existence of this substance, then, it ought to be easy to define a stationary point. Such a point would not be moving with respect to the lumeniferous ether. This could be detected by observing the speed of light arriving from various different directions. If the speeds were all the same, then the point in question ought to be stationary with respect to the ether.

If you had high-school physics, you have probably done these ether experiments. The light speed was checked as it arrived from a particular star at different times of the day and year and in every case the speed of the incident light was exactly the same. There was not even the slightest bit of difference that could be attributable to the movement of the Earth around the sun, or to the rotation of the Earth on its own axis.

Scientists could not accept the notion that their laboratory was an absolutely stationary point in space. Therefore they postulated that there was an "ether wind" such that the Earth carried ether along with it, much as it carries along its own atmosphere. This would explain the observations. But it also wrecked the purpose for which the experiments had been attempted in the first place: to find an absolutely stationary reference frame for the universe. If the Earth carries its own ether, and the ether is in fact "windy," then it cannot be used as a satisfactory means of finding an absolutely stationary point. The project was abandoned. When Einstein "changed" physics by postulating that the speed of light would always appear to be the same no matter from what point of view it is measured, the pursuit of finding an absolutely stationary point was given up altogether. Evidently, motion is definable only in a relative sense. Any point, be it a real object or a mathematically determined position in space, can be used as a reference but none are absolute.

## Absolute Acceleration

While it is difficult to determine whether an object is moving or not or what true position it is in, we *can* determine whether or not there is acceleration and in what direction this change of velocity is taking place.

Acceleration is defined as a change in *velocity*. Velocity consists of speed and direction. If either the speed or the direction changes, the result is acceleration. Acceleration can be measured in terms of the force it causes on an object having a certain mass. An acceleration of about 9.8 meters per second per second (9.8 m/s$^2$), or 32 feet per second per second, creates a force of one *gravity* (1 g). This rate of acceleration is the change in speed for a free-falling object in the gravitational field of Earth.

The acceleration of an object can be deemed zero if there is no force exerted on that object. A device for measuring acceleration might consist of a weight supported by six springs inside a cubical enclosure (Fig. 3-3). Say this device was put in a situation where the acceleration is 0 g, such as in orbit around the Earth or coasting in free space, and the springs were adjusted so that the weight is suspended in the exact center of the cube. A force in any direction would then cause the weight to be displaced from the center of the cube in that direction. The greater the force, the more the displacement, and the farther off center the weight will be.

If this three-dimensional acceleration meter is taken from orbit or from its coasting path in free space and is placed on the surface of the Earth, the weight would be displaced toward the center of the earth. You could calibrate the instrument by marking this displacement as 9.8 m/s$^2$.

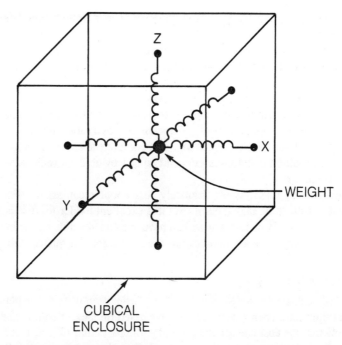

**Fig. 3-3.** An accelerometer could be constructed with a weight and six springs in a cube. Axes are depicted by X, Y and Z, all mutually orthogonal.

There are other ways that such a displacement can be created. Say the instrument is subjected to an ever-increasing straight-line speed in outer space (like the feeling you experience when accelerating in an automobile or airplane). Or, say the instrument is swung around and around in a circle, again in outer space to avoid the effects of the gravitational field of the Earth. If this acceleration is continuous, there is a constant force opposite the direction of the acceleration. If the acceleration is always exactly $9.8$ m/s$^2$, then the opposing force is always the same. If the instrument is subjected to the gravitation of the Earth or to some other constant acceleration of $9.8$ m/s$^2$, the two will be indistinguishable from one another. That is, in terms of their effect, the gravitation and the speed/direction change are exactly the same thing.

The acceleration meter always displays either some finite acceleration, indicated by displacement of the weight, or no acceleration, indicated by exact centering of the weight. It might be thought of as an indicator of absolute acceleration because it functions no matter where it is in the entire universe. Absolute acceleration, then, can be considered definable.

Interestingly, we do not think of ourselves, as we stand on the surface of our planet, as accelerating straight upward at $9.8$ m/s$^2$. In a strictly physics-oriented sense, however, we are doing just that, and the effect on time-space is exactly as if we were doing that. This is the basis for Einstein's general theory of relativity, a theory that takes the acceleration of reference points into account. The general theory was developed to overcome some of the paradoxes of the special theory, such as the twin paradox. The twin paradox is where twins Jim and Joe might differ in age by some specific amount both ways at once; for example,

Jim might be a year older than Joe and also a year younger, despite having been born on the exact same day.*

The absolute acceleration of an object allowed to "go wherever it wants" in free space without resistance in the form of atmospheric drag, water drag, or other obstruction is always zero. Examples of such conditions are orbit around the Earth, the sun, or the center of the galaxy or coasting among the stars. Any such object has an absolute acceleration of zero. As such, acceleration can be regarded as not depending on any other things in the universe; it can be determined entirely by means of observation made on, or in, the object in question. No comparison is necessary. The complete absence of force—centering of the weight—is a condition that does not depend on nearby objects, reference frames, or anything else whatsoever.

This concept, all by itself, is unfortunately just about meaningless. For practical application, there is little to be said about it. But it is excellent fodder for discussion about the nature of this universe. How is it that we can have such an absolute that is immediately discernible no matter where we are in a cosmos we are taught is a relative thing?

## The Totality of All Things

When the last section concluded that absolute acceleration does not depend on any other things, it might have been a hasty conclusion based on lack of complete evidence. How do we know that the absolute acceleration of some particular object, like a car on a highway, is not dependent on all the stars in the whole universe? It seems ridiculous to think that all of those distant atoms might have anything to do with the acceleration of a car on Route 1 between Richmond and Washington, D.C. But we cannot really say that the acceleration is *not* dependent on all of the rest of the matter in the universe quite simply because we are not able to remove the rest of this matter and make a comparison.

Suppose all the rest of the universe were to disappear except for our solar system. Would the same forces remain for the various changes in velocity? It is impossible to know for sure, but here are some theoretical hypotheses.

In a universe with nothing but itself — a closed-off space with just one object in it — there would be nothing with which motion could be compared. This would also be true for rotation. There would be no reference that might allow a unit to say, "I'm rotating," or "I'm changing speed." All motion and therefore all changes in motion would be without any means for determination. Then, there could be no force accompanying acceleration because there could be no such thing as acceleration. Determination of position would likewise have no meaning.

Suppose just yourself, a ball, and a string existed in some closed universe (Fig. 3-4). As you hold the ball and string, this apparatus floats out away from you because there is no gravity. What would happen if you swung the ball and string around and around your head? Would the ball stretch out the string, and describe circles around you with a radius equal to the length of the string? If this experiment was attempted on the moon, on Mars, in outer space, or anywhere in our own universe, that is probably what would happen. But what about a universe in which there are no distant stars, no other planets, or even an Earth with which to determine rotation? How could you cause the ball to go "around and

---

*This paradox is discussed in the first book in this series, *Puzzles, Paradoxes and Brain Teasers* (Blue Ridge Summit: TAB BOOKS, 1988): 71-2.

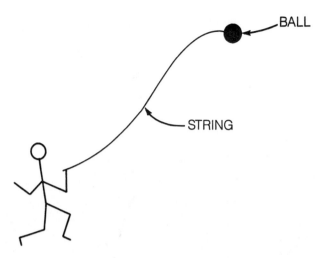

**Fig. 3-4.** Say you found yourself suspended alone in a universe with a ball and string. How will you determine motion?

around" when there are no points of reference? If you were all alone in a closed universe with a ball and string, the only reference would be your own body. This would be by far the greatest portion of the mass in the universe, the ball and string accounting for just a little.

Let's surmise that if the ball and string *did* stretch out and describe circles when you swung it around, then you could get it to do the same thing just by turning yourself on the axis of your own body. Or, putting it another way, swinging the ball around yourself would be the same thing as swinging yourself around the ball. These two things would in fact be identical if the ball were as massive as your body — say, a large lead sphere of mass 80 kilograms. With no other masses in a universe to determine comparative motion, there can be no acceleration and should be no resulting forces.

Suppose now that you get into a closed universe with the same ball and string and one companion. The two of you float some distance apart, say 10 body lengths (the body length is the standard unit of distance in your universe; you could also use string lengths or ball diameters). There are various possibilities, now, for determining acceleration. The two of you might be moving or rotating relative to each other; the ball could be just floating somewhere near you in space with the string slack. This view of things is consistent from all reference frames (Fig. 3-5A).

Suppose now that you swing the ball around and around your body. The ball now seems to be rotating with respect to both you and your companion, and the string goes taut because of acceleration force (Fig. 3-5B). The exact amount of force on the string is not clear; it will probably differ from that in our universe because there is less total mass in the closed universe. However, if a vote was taken among the scientists and mathematicians of the world in this situation, it's a good bet that the taut-string model would win cleanly.

Now suppose that you begin to tumble along with the ball revolving around you. Thus, you no longer perceive the ball as going around your body, but instead you see it standing still some distance from you, and your companion, several body lengths distant,

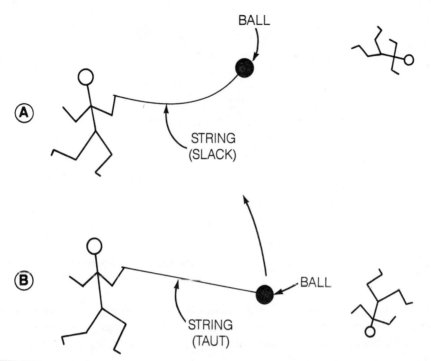

**Fig. 3-5.** You and a partner, suspended in a void, try to determine absolute rotation. At (A), you hold the ball and string. The string is slack. When you swing the ball around you (B), the string becomes taut.

appears to be tumbling. The companion likewise sees you tumbling, along with the ball and string. Question: Is the string now taut? Is there a force on it? Suppose you and the ball and string together have the same mass as your partner. Which point of view, then, is correct? Either there is force on the string, or there is not; and this truth does not change simply depending on where the video camera is. The two renditions of this situation are shown in Fig. 3-6 A and B. It's not certain whether it will be pulled taut or not, and there is no way to check this in reality. Our universe contains trillions of stars and a tremendous total mass. It would be immediately clear in our real cosmos which situation is correct.

In any universe, regardless of how many different objects it might contain, there is one, and only one, set of truths. Whether or not all of these truths are discernible varies depending on the particular universe. But either the ball pulls the string taut or it does not; both situations cannot exist at the same time.

The absoluteness of acceleration in our universe is apparently the result of the total action of all things in the cosmos. Every particle, however distant, contributes its effect to the inertial forces present on a car on Route 1 and on everything else. This is not so difficult to accept from a theoretical standpoint when you realize that the gravitational influence of every object, from the largest quasar down to the smallest sub-atom, extends indefinitely into space around that object. Although the gravitational effect of a quark some 100 million light years distant is extremely small, it nonetheless does exist — and taking away that quark would affect the entire universe, even if to a miniscule degree.

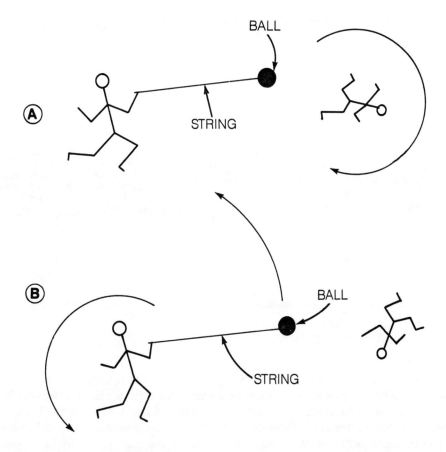

**Fig. 3-6.** Two different ways of looking at rotation. At (A), your partner seems to be tumbling. At (B), you and the ball and string are tumbling. These views are equivalent if there is nothing else in the universe.

## The Center of the Universe

There might be a geometric center to the universe. If this is true, then the universe is finite. An absolute position could be determined for any object if we knew the geometric center of the universe, assuming this central point actually lies in the universe.

It might seem trivial that if there is a center of the universe, then that center ought to lie in the universe. But this is not to be taken for granted; in fact, according to a popular model of the universe, there is a central point removed from the actual geometry of the continuum of space as we perceive it. A dimensionally reduced illustration of this situation is shown in Fig. 3-7.

In the model of Fig. 3-7, the universe is the surface of a four-dimensional sphere. For lack of a specific name, let us call this object a *tetroid*. Beginning in any direction, the path of a photon through three-space will eventually return to the starting point from the opposite direction. This is true for every point on the three-dimensional surface of the tetroid. This surface is perceived as "space." But the center point of the tetroid is not in our "space" at all. The only way to arrive at the central point in the universe would be to find a way to travel in four dimensions.

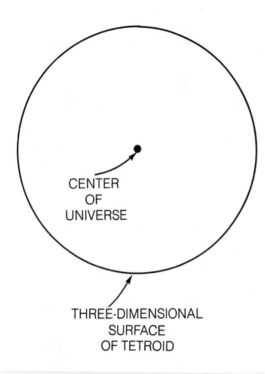

CENTER
OF
UNIVERSE

THREE-DIMENSIONAL
SURFACE
OF TETROID

**Fig. 3-7.** If the universe is a four-dimensional sphere (tetroid) on which we exist in three dimensions, then the center of the universe is not in our reach.

What is the fourth dimension? Many say it is time. In fact, using time as a fourth dimension produces a meaningful model for a time-space universe. Einstein was the first to rigorously define this time-space. However, consider a fourth dimension as being yet another spatial dimension, a dimension we cannot perceive directly but must instead depict by mathematical means. A four-space is a space that requires exactly four coordinates to uniquely define the position of a point. These coordinates might be three space coordinates $(x, y, z)$ and time $t$, or they might all be space coordinates $(w, x, y, z)$. It is helpful to define a fourth dimension as a spatial dimension independent of time because this allows consideration of the existence of universes having any number of dimensions.

Absolute position in space might be depicted by choosing some point, say our own solar system, as one pole and then describing the position of any other point by means of three angular coordinates. The "equator" would be a plane surface equidistant from our solar system and the counterpole on the tetroid. The angular coordinates would be defined with respect to the center point of the tetroid. (I cannot provide an illustration of this situation since it is four-dimensional in its entirety. Nonetheless, its mathematical definition is sound.)

Many astronomers today believe that our universe is tetroidal in shape. Therefore, it does indeed have a center, and absolute position can be defined with respect to this center if one is willing to make the mildly egotistical choice of having our solar system be at one pole of the surface of the tetroid. It might at first seem that this is trivial, a reversion to the ancient theory that we are at the center of the universe or that we occupy some exalted position in the cosmos. This is, in fact, no more true than to say that the north or south pole are exalted places on the Earth—a statement that, I am fairly sure, would be called ridiculous by anyone who has ever set foot on either spot.

# CHAPTER 4

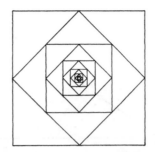

# Cause/Effect, Coincidence, and Predestiny

IT HAS BEEN SAID THAT EVERY EVENT HAS A CAUSE. NOTHING HAPPENS WITHOUT A REA-son. This argument has been used as a proof for the existence of God. Because we obviously exist and a universe exists in which we live, there must be some cause for the existence of it all. This has generally been thought of as a single, prime cause, the original reason for all events that take place in the cosmos. Is this a valid idea? Might there be more than one "prime mover?" Or is it possible that there is no such thing as a "prime mover," and that time goes in circles?

The idea of a "prime mover" is illustrated in Fig. 4-1. Events are shown as occurring like a tree branching out. The trunk of this tree is the "prime mover." The "prime mover" of an event is found by tracing its cause and finding the cause for this cause and so on until you can go no further.

This ancient line of reasoning is faulty in various ways. First, there is no guarantee that you can always trace things back, getting stuck somewhere before arriving at the original cause of all events. Moreover, effects are not always causes, nor are causes effects. When discovering a cause for something, it is not necessarily certain what will result. There might be more than one effect from the event under scrutiny. This can be illustrated as the branching of the tree (Fig. 4-2A).

Another reason the "prime mover" theory is faulty is the possibility that a single event could have more than one cause (Fig. 4-2B). This is probably the rule instead of the exception. As an example, suppose your house burns down while you are on vacation. You come home to find nothing except a pile of rubble. The facts begin to emerge: the oven was left on and no one had seen the smoke to call the fire department when the house caught fire. There were several cans of gasoline in the garage for use with the lawn mower. The electric wiring in the house had long been suspect. The door had been left unlocked. Finally it is determined that the fire did indeed start in the kitchen, but not near the oven. It was somewhere in the electrical wiring in one of the kitchen walls.

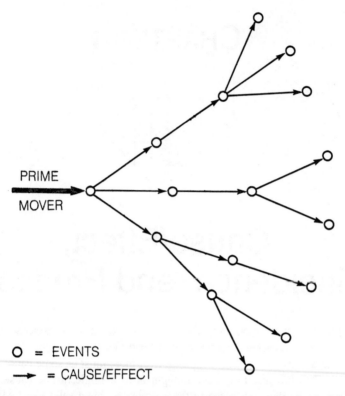

O = EVENTS

→ = CAUSE/EFFECT

**Fig. 4-1.** Illustration of the "prime mover" theory, where all effects are the result of a single original effect.

What was *the* single cause for the house burning down? Was it the bad wiring, or was it the fact that the oven was left on (the fire occurred in the wiring for that particular appliance)? Or was it the fact that no one called the fire department soon enough to prevent complete destruction of the house? If the door was unlocked, it could have been arson, although that possibility appears to have been ruled out. The gas cans in the garage probably blew up once the fire got near them, accelerating the fire's progress.

There really isn't one particular single cause for the event here, as it usually is in real life. There are almost always several reasons, not just one reason, for something to happen. This might have been the situation when the Creation itself took place—if there was a Creation that can be identified as a single event. Some scientists still differ with that belief.

## Past Dictates Future

It is often said that "what happens in the future depends on what has already taken place in the past." This is true to a certain extent. Most things don't just happen at random. If the temperature of the Sun were to increase by a few percent, the climatic change on the Earth would be inevitable. If there is a strong cold front pushing down through Iowa in June, there will quite possibly be heavy thundershowers associated with it. We can

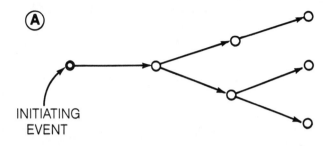

INITIATING
EVENT

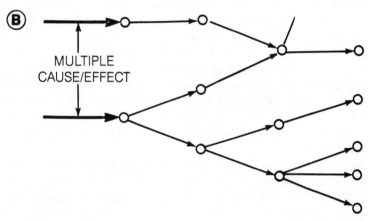

MULTIPLE
CAUSE/EFFECT

Fig. 4-2. At (A), a single event results in more than one effect; at (B), multiple effects produce a single result.

actually make certain predictions based on what we know about the past, and this is itself an example of the truth of that saying: Past events affect future predictions.

To what extent is the future determined by events past? Some say completely; nothing happens without a cause, and all of the causes for future events must be in the past. It helps if we illustrate past, present, and future by means of a time line as shown in Fig. 4-3. The present is indicated by a point that has no duration, or if you prefer, has sufficient duration for our minds to realize that we exist. (That's a few hundredths of a second.) The past is that time period to the left of the point, and the future is shown to the right of the point. Even a few milliseconds to the right of the point is a moment in the future, and a point just a few milliseconds to the left is in the past.

The structure of the universe is such that time seems to "flow" so that the point indicating the present moves along the time line towards the right. Any point in the future will eventually become a point in the past if you are willing to wait for it. This is true regardless of whether that point is one second away, one hour away, one week away, or one year away. It is even true for some point 100 years away. There is reason to believe that it might

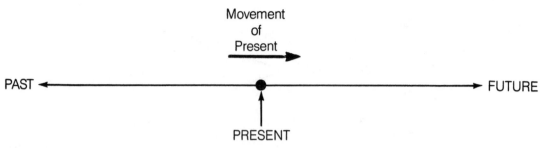

**Fig. 4-3.** The traditional time line, where the present "flows" toward the future.

not hold strictly true for extremely large intervals of time, but for the moment do not be concerned with that realm.

Think of the line moving toward the left, with the point of the present standing still. Both of those ideas are essentially the same concept. Dividing the line into equal-sized intervals, each interval represents a certain standard unit of time, for example, one second. The length of one second can be very accurately determined by measuring the vibrations of a quartz crystal or the oscillations of certain atoms of matter. This is how the National Bureau of Standards does it. The universe has an abundance of little time standards such as the solar day (24 hours), the sidereal or star day (23 hours, 56 minutes), and the year (about 365 1/4 solar days or 366 1/4 sidereal days). Or, consider the time it takes for the Solar System to traverse one complete circle around the center of our Galaxy; this is literally millions of years.

Why time seems to "flow" along this line is the subject for much scientific and even philosophical debate. Scientists are apt to call time a dimension, and its passage is only an illusion created by the fact that our access to this dimension is limited. (We live, in a sense, in a three-and-a-half-dimensional cosmos.) Some scientists consider time an entity apart from the spatial dimensions. The rate at which time "flows" was long believed to be a constant. In fact, the famous mathematician and physicist Isaac Newton stated this directly. It has since been shown, mathematically and empirically, that the rate of time flow is not constant but depends on motion and acceleration. And if this is not bizarre enough, there is some mathematical evidence to suggest that even the direction in which time progresses can be reversed. Some high-speed particles, at least in theory, move backward in time. This idea gives rise to the strange nature of time travel, a subject familiar to any well-read science-fiction enthusiast.

If the future is determined entirely by past events, then at any given moment, there exists a set of potential causes X to the left of the "present" point on the time line and a set of effects Y to the right of the point (see Fig. 4-4). If the future is entirely dictated by past events, then for every event Y there must be at least one cause X. No event Y occurs without some cause X that may or may not be identifiable. This theory might be called the Marionette Theory, which implies that every one of us is a puppet of fate. The strings are all pulled by fate (or God, if you care to think of fate that way, or God and Satan, or some mad scientist in a great laboratory in the seventh dimension, etc.). Whether or not fate directly controls every single event is not of much importance in this theory. The fact is that if this theory is true, then there must be at least one "prime mover" behind everything that happens or will happen.

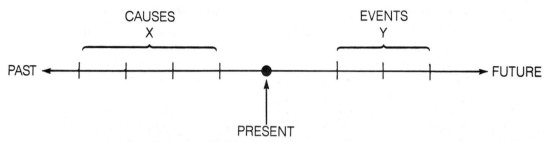

**Fig. 4-4.** Causes (X) can be thought of as existing in the past and events or results (Y) are in the future.

Because it seems to eliminate free choice as a factor in the events of the universe, this theory is not appealing to many people. Try to evaluate things from a logical point of view, however, without allowing our preferences to get in the way. In any case, reality is as it is whether we happen to like it or not. With this in mind, it is safe to conclude that there is evidence both in favor of and against the Marionette Theory.

Consider that no future event could occur without some past to come from. In this sense, if you search hard and long enough, you ought to be able to find all of the forces at work and perhaps predict the position of every atom in the whole universe at some particular time, say, 10 seconds from now. This would require an enormous computer, but if the number of particles in the cosmos is finite (and this is thought by many astrophysicists to be the case), then it should be possible to enumerate the behavior of each and every one of them.

If the future is in fact the result of past events, there is no way to determine every future event based on the past. This notion arises from Kurt Godel's Incompleteness Theorem. Kurt Godel, a logician, proved that in first-order logic, there are some statements that cannot be proven either true or false from the axioms of the system. Our universe must be much more complicated than first-order logic. Therefore, in the real cosmos, there must be some things that might happen, but we cannot prove whether or not they will. The reason this cannot be proven one way or the other is not because of the sheer complexity of the universe but some other factor, an uncertainty factor—the incompleteness of truth itself. This leaves room for the possibility that even if things are predetermined, it is impossible to predict all events in the future. This leaves room for wonder and hope. If someone comes along and says that you will die in exactly thirty days, three hours, and three minutes, you can have faith in the Incompleteness Theorem to guarantee that this person is not necessarily correct, no matter how sophisticated or convincing the argument might be.

It is also possible that some things happen spontaneously, with no cause at all. This was in fact an axiom in the now more-or-less-defunct "Steady State" theory of the origin and evolution of the universe. According to this theory, new matter is constantly being created in the universe from nothing. This happens at a constant rate, and uniformly throughout the whole of space. No reason is given for this continuous creation of matter; it was just hypothesized to account for the apparent fact that the universe is growing. All distant galaxies appear to be receding from our Milky Way. The farther away a galaxy is, the faster its recession speed seems to be. This is determined by observing the spectra of the stars in these galaxies. The lines in the spectra, caused by absorption of energy at various wavelengths, are displaced toward the red end (the so-called red shift), and this has been attributed to the Doppler effect. It is thought that the actual fiber of space is expanding, and all of the matter in the cosmos is being carried along in this expansion. New matter is formed to keep the density of the universe constant, in spite of the expansion. What would cause this to happen? The proponents of the Steady State theory (and there still are some) give no reason except that it must be happening if we are to believe what we see. Continuous creation is, for them, no more of a hurdle than a single event of huge proportions. No cause is given for either the original creation in the more popular "Big Bang" theory or the Steady State's continuous creation. Oh, there must be some reason, the scientists say, but it is not up to us to figure out exactly what it is.

Theologians take this opportunity to exclaim, "We know the reason!" Of course, when many come up against a wall in their minds, they can always jump over that wall by invoking God. God is played like a trump card. He's awfully convenient, that God. It may well be, however, that even the original creation of the Big Bang was the result of one or more events that occurred in some other universe and can be explained quite naturally in those terms. The problem is that we have no way of knowing what that event might have been. The equations don't give us any hint; they just indicate that there was nothing at all in the cosmos before the Big Bang. No one seriously wants to believe that all of the matter in the universe simply came into being without a reason.

## Future Dictates Past

Some attach bizarre explanations to events to be able to say, "what will happen in the *future* determines what already has happened in the *past*." Suppose you are not certain whether you should get the car washed or not. You don't want to wash the car before you leave on a trip if it is going to rain. If it's going to be good weather, you do want to wash the car.

All the time you think about this, the air masses over the countryside are mingling with one another, and the recipe for the weather scenario is being set for later in the day when you plan to leave on your trip. The events going on right then, as you are deciding whether you ought to wash the car or not, are determining what the weather will be like. The possibility of rain is already "in the cards," so to speak. Either it will rain or it will not. You listen to the weather forecast, but meteorologists are not always right. They say it will probably not rain—the precipitation probability is 20 percent—so you get the car washed. Ten minutes after you hit the highway, you run right into a severe thunderstorm and all of your efforts go for nought.

You might argue that had you not been going to wash the car (in the future, as you pondered the decision), then the air masses would have behaved differently prior to your decision and there would have been no rain. This might be called "supreme cosmic paranoia." The events in the universe are so constructed so as to inconvenience *you*. "Who is this man, that even the winds and seas conspire to defy him?" I have heard people jokingly talk like this, as if the whole universe were arranged around the "victim" to the extent that cause and effect might even operate backwards in time so as to ensure that someone is made miserable.

Can such cause/effect situations really occur? Can future events or circumstances actually have an effect on what has already taken place? Your first thought might be, "No way. That would be like backward time travel, and backward time travel is impossible because it results in a contradiction." But perhaps things are not that simple.

You have probably heard the argument that is used against backward time travel. You could travel back in time and kill your own mother before you were born. Then that would prevent your birth, so your mother would not have been killed, so you then would have been born, and would have killed her, preventing your having been born, et cetera, *ad nauseum*. There hasn't yet been an attempt to travel backward in time with serious intent, but certain particles known as *tachyons* might move in time in the opposite direction from what we consider "forward."

The crux of the argument is this question: To what extent are cosmic events tied together? It might be that future events can be interrelated with past events in cause/effect ways of which we are completely ignorant. This is not really equivalent to backward time travel. It does, however, say something about fate.

Is the future predestined? If so, then a "change" in future events can cause a change in past events as compared with what would have been true if things were left alone. If time is a dimension, then the whole universe—past, present and future—becomes one fixed, four-dimensional "mural" that is all constructed in one single, particular way. Events in the future are then just as solidly molded as those in the past; people are just not *aware* of future events in as much detail as past events. In such a universe, an alteration in one part of the "mural" might cause a change in the entire picture—past, present and future—even if that change were made in the future. Then you could say that future events have some effect on past ones! We simply cannot figure out precisely what all of these effects are because we are not totally aware of the details of the future.

Another way to look at this is to imagine the universe as a mobile (Fig. 4-5). In this mobile, all of the parts are evenly balanced. The true cosmos is a four-dimensional mobile in this model, because time is treated as a dimension. If the position of any of the constituents of the mobile changes, all of the other parts will move in order to bring the mobile back into balance. This will occur no matter which constituent of the mobile moves. The constituent moved might be in the past, present, or future. It is fairly easy to see how changing history might affect the future. (For example, what would have happened if the Nazis had developed the atomic bomb before the United States did?) It is even easy to see how present events can influence the future. But it is still a hurdle of the imagination to envision a change of future events having an effect on the past. In the mobile model, the future is predestined in the sense that "whatever will be, will be." All of the parts of the four-dimensional mobile are already there; some of them just haven't been seen yet.

## Predestiny and Free Choice

The notion that the future is predestined bothers many people because it gives the impression that none of us have any choice concerning what happens. To some extent, we do have choice. That is plain enough. You can choose, for example, whether or not you want to get drunk tonight. You might not have much choice, however, whether or not you get caught if you also decide to drive while drunk. However, either you will get drunk tonight or you won't. Or maybe you'll just get halfway drunk. The point is that whatever

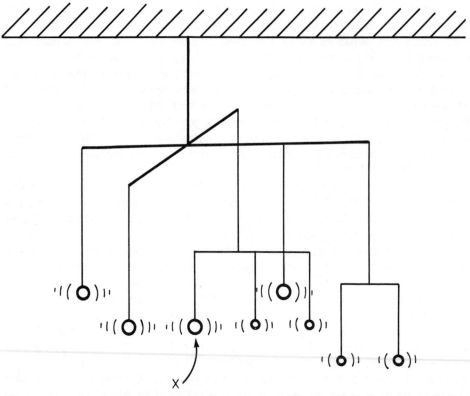

**Fig. 4-5.** The mobile theory, where events are likened to the objects in a mobile. If one object, say X, is upset, then the whole balance is changed.

will be, will be. Even if you have a choice in some matters, the choice you make is already in existence according to the four-dimensional-mobile model of the universe.

Some scientists—most of them, in fact—consider time to be a fourth dimension. This is because it has the properties that dimensions "should" have. However, there is some argument that time is a phenomenon independent of dimensions. The number of spatial dimensions is generally determined by finding out how many coordinates are needed to uniquely define a point in that space. In our universe, that number is three. The coordinate for time uniquely defines when an event takes place with respect to a certain frame of reference such as the new year or the birth of Christ. It is thought that the whole fiber of the cosmos is a vast network of spaces like a polydimensional foam of which our universe is a single bubble that happens to contain three spatial dimensions. Some universes could have less than three dimensions and some could have more up to a possible 11 dimensions according to some modern theoreticians.

But suppose time is a thread that runs through all of the different bubbles in the "foam cosmos" in the same manner for an 11-dimensioned universe or a two-dimensioned one as it does for ours. Time might not be a dimension in the true sense, and the mobile model might not really be a good indicator of the nature of time-space. If this is true, then the future just might be up to chance, with little or no predestiny involved. Even if this is the case, however, the proposition "whatever will be, will be" holds. It is true all by itself.

Either an event will occur, or it will not. There is no halfway. As far as we know, once something has occurred in this particular universe, that event is set in the fiber of time-space for all time. There is no way to go back and change it.

People are in fact quite surprised when they find out how little freedom of choice there really is in the course of events. The annoyance caused by a lack of freedom is largely from simply being aware of that restriction. You won't fear captivity if you're not aware that you're being held captive. Yet, for the time being, everyone is a prisoner on Planet Earth. You cannot simply pack up and go somewhere else. Further, many are essentially restricted to the country in which they live. Often, economic factors limit the freedom to do various things.

## Coincidence

The word "coincidence" means "condition of coinciding." It is an often-misused word. When most people use the word "coincidence," they really mean that it is an unusual event, a rarity, a random fluke. A coincidence in the true sense happens when apparently unrelated events happen at the same time as if they are in fact related when there is no apparent reason why they should be related.

Sometimes coincidences simply happen out of the clear blue. Other times, there is a hidden causal relationship between the events. For the events X and Y, say they have a causal relationship of the form X causes Y (Fig. 4-6A), Y causes X (Fig. 4-6B), or Z (some other event) might cause both X and Y (Fig. 4-6C). The simple occurrence of the coincidence does not immediately make clear which of these three situations, if any, is the case.

Suppose a tornado strikes the same house three times on the same day in three consecutive years. Now there's a coincidence! The house is rebuilt exactly the same as it was before, after being hit, say, on June 11, 1985. Then it is struck again on June 11, 1986. Again it is rebuilt just the same way as before. On June 11, 1987, sure enough, another pile of rubble is deposited where the house was. What would you do if you owned that house? (I can tell you what I'd do.) Maybe you'd build it with a different floor plan or sell the lot to someone else. Perhaps the geography of the area is such that tornadoes are directed toward the place where the house is. But maybe it's just in the stacks of fate that you are to be plagued with tornadoes for your whole life it it's you who has been so unlucky as to have had this experience. Whenever a thing like this happens, people are likely to look for a cause. There is a cause, of course, but it is probably pure coincidence, a sheer fluke of fate. I can recall reading about someone who had been in houses demolished by tornadoes on something like seven different occasions. The poor victim was inclined to think that the gods were after him. Others thought he was lucky *not* to have been killed. One man had been hit directly by lightning several times and had survived each strike. The reason things like this happen is probably just that there are so many people, and so much time, that eventually things of that sort are likely to happen.

Do not make the error of thinking, however, that a certain strange event "comes due" as time passes. If you flip a coin over and over, for example, you will eventually get three "heads" in a row. It isn't generally necessary to flip the coin very many times before this actually does happen. But the chances of it occurring on any three given tosses can be calculated as $P = (0.5)(0.5)(0.5) = 0.125$ or 12.5 percent. This is always the case. It

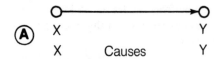

(A) X     Y

 X  Causes  Y

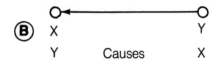

(B) X     Y

 Y  Causes  X

**Fig. 4-6.** Three possibilities for events X and Y occurring simultaneously. At (A), X causes Y. At (B), Y causes X. At (C), Z causes both X and Y.

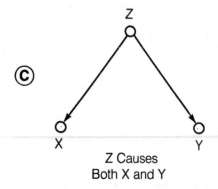

(C)

Z

X    Y

Z Causes
Both X and Y

doesn't increase after ten tries, or a hundred, or even a million unsuccessful attempts. Nor does the chance of a house getting hit by a tornado get any less if it is demolished once, or twice, or three times. Probabilities are exactly that: mathematical chances.

However, there is a fundamental difference between the chances of a coin coming up "heads" three times in a row and natural events such as tornadoes destroying buildings. The chances of getting three "heads" in a row are one in eight, or 12.5 percent. This can be evaluated by doing controlled experiments. If a coin is made so that its mass is uniformly distributed in the form of a disk (in reality this is not quite true, but it is pretty close with most coins), then the chances of its coming up "heads" are exactly 50:50 on any single toss. This is verified by flipping the coin dozens, hundreds, thousands, or even millions of times. As the number of tosses increases, the number of "heads" and the number of "tails" tosses approaches a 1:1 ratio. A possible graph of such a ratio, as the number of tosses is increased, is shown in Fig. 4-7. Note that the first five tosses are all "heads." But after a few dozens tosses, the ratio is much more nearly 1:1. At some future points, actually at an infinite number of them in the mathematical sense, the ratio will be exactly 1:1. For example, you might get to a point where you have flipped 23,566 "heads" and 23,566 "tails."

But with a natural event such as a tornado, controlled experiments are not possible. The probability can't really be determined that a given house will be hit by a tornado on a

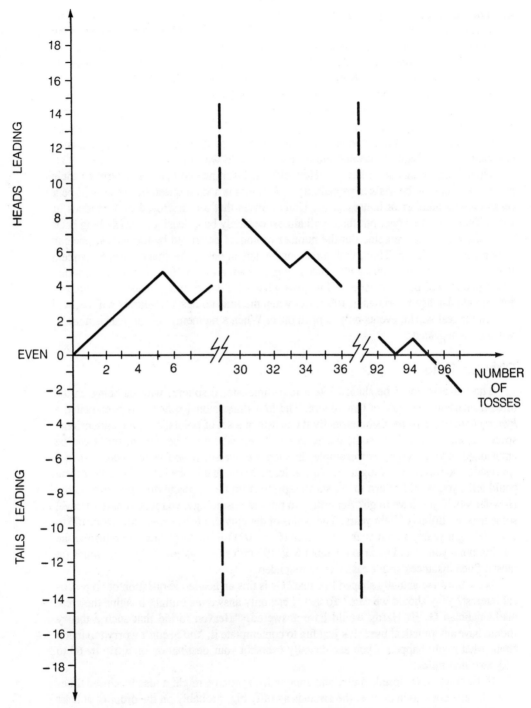

**Fig. 4-7.** The tossing of a coin graphed in terms of heads leading tails and vice versa. The graph always converges toward the even (zero) line, although it might in theory stray as far away as the number of tosses.

given day, during a given year, or even in the course of the house's existence. Such events are one-shot deals. We do not have access to, say, $10^{15}$ identical universes to see how many of them would allow for the demolition of a certain house by a tornado in a certain year. If there were $10^{15}$ (a quadrillion) identical universes, you might observe a given house get blown away in perhaps 34 of them during the year 1999. Nevertheless, there is only one universe at our disposal, and the house will either get blown away in 1999, or it will not. Someone can invest money in that house with the faith that it will "probably" be spared, but even this use of the word "probably" is imprecise. The investor doesn't *think* such an event will happen (or he/she should hope not, unless trying to defraud some insurance company), but probability has nothing whatsoever to do with it.

Now I hear someone thinking, "How else do insurance companies determine their premiums if not on the basis of probability?" And that is a valid question. There will be a certain actual number of houses in the United States that are destroyed by tornadoes in 1999. There may be none, but there will almost certainly be at least a few. Looking back over past years and averaging out the number of houses destroyed by tornadoes, one can obtain a median figure. Then, with a real mathematical basis, the chances are 50 percent that there will be more houses than that average blown away in 1999 and 50 percent that fewer houses will be demolished. This gives a basis for determining insurance premiums for tornado damage to houses in 1999. But when the time comes, "whatever will be, will be." In the real world, events only happen once. When a moment, day, or year is gone, it will not be repeated.

## Circular Time

The universe could be shaped like a four-dimensional sphere, with us being on the three-dimensional surface of that sphere. The four-dimensional sphere has been called a *hypersphere* or a *tetroid*. Geometrically it consists of a set of points in a four-dimensional space, all equidistant from some center point. A tetroid cannot be drawn, but it can be envisioned in some ways. For example, in such a universe, if you were to take off in a spaceship and travel in a straight line (or, at least, a line that looked straight as far as you could tell), you would return to the starting place from the opposite direction eventually. How far would you have to go? According to present cosmology, you would have to travel some tens of billions of light years. The radius of the universe is believed to be from $10^{10}$ to $2 \times 10^{10}$ light years; a light year is 6 trillion ($6 \times 10^{12}$) miles. So in order to return to the starting point you would need to go about $6 \times 10^{22}$ miles (at least) or $1.2 \times 10^{23}$ miles (at most). Such distances aren't easily comprehended.

Is the universe actually shaped like that? Or is this an academic question of no practical interest? Why should we care? To that, I can only answer as I might imagine the great mathematician G. H. Hardy would have answered: "Heaven forbid that such a theory should have any practical use." It's just fun to contemplate it. You needn't worry too much about what might happen if you accidentally overshot your destination on a trip by 60 to 120 sextillion miles.

If the universe is closed, finite, and unbounded spatially, might it also be closed time-wise? If time does go in circles, the circle is awfully big, probably on the order of at least $10^{10}$ years in circumference. We can observe spatial curvature by observing the light from distant stars as it passes close to the sun. The sun has a strong gravitational field and this

66

gravitation causes the light rays to be deflected (Fig. 4-8). This is not simply a bending of the light rays caused by an attractive force against the photons as they move like pellets from a shotgun. Light *always* travels the shortest distance between two points. Therefore, a gravitational field causes the shortest distance between two points to be along a different path than it is in the absence of gravitation. Space becomes non-Euclidean when there is gravitation. That means the simple geometric laws of Euclid, the ones you learned in high school by rote, do not apply. They *almost* apply, and can be considered true in very small regions of space, but on a grander scale the difference becomes considerable. Gravitation exists to some extent everywhere in the universe, even in the intergalactic voids. The net effect is to bend space into a four-dimensional hypersphere or tetroid.

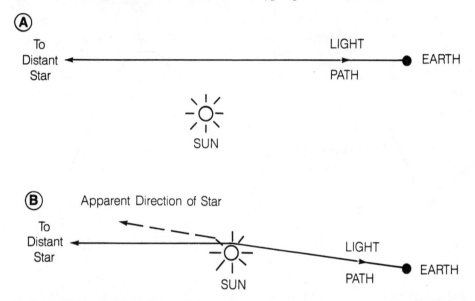

**Fig. 4-8.** (A) illustrates that light from a distant star is unaffected when it does not pass near the sun. At (B), as the light from a distant star grazes the sun, it is bent by the sun's gravitation.

This concept of the tetroid then yields a cosmological model in which the whole universe was originally born in a violent explosion from a single geometric point and took the form of an expanding tetroid on the surface of which the galaxies, quasars, stars, planets, and all the other objects in space seen and unseen, evolved. The radiation from this fireball is still detected as a faint background noise coming from all directions in space. This background noise, indicating a present temperature of three degrees Kelvin (just about five degrees Fahrenheit above absolute zero), was first discovered by accident in the Bell Telephone Laboratories.

Will the universe continue to expand and cool off, finally dying in darkness and cold? Or will gravitation pull all the matter back again eventually, ending the universe like a backward replay of its birth? Scientists do not know for certain. The density of the universe is the key, and according to what we can see, there is not enough matter to pull it back together again, ever. But we are just beginning to learn that much of the matter in the cosmos—most of it, perhaps—is invisible. If this is so, it is possible that there will be a final collapse. It will be many billions of years in the future, but it will come if there is sufficient matter. Then the question becomes, what after that? Another explosion? This is the "oscillating universe" theory. Perhaps the matter will collapse through a single point and emerge as antimatter in the next cycle. Or maybe the next cycle will take the same form as this cycle. It seems logical enough to think that the next cycle would require the same length of time to be completed as this one, and would yield a cosmos of the same maximum size with the same course of evolution, like the next cycle of a sine wave (Fig. 4-9). This, of course, is speculation, but for the time being there is not much else we can do.

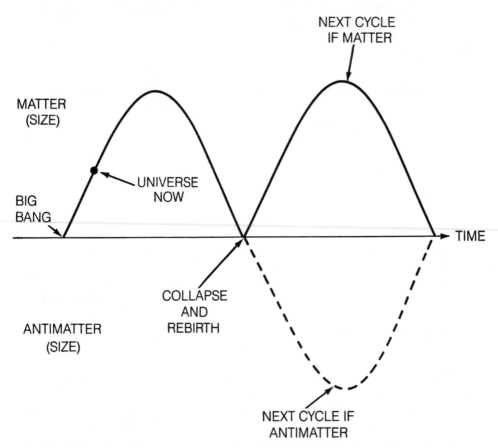

**Fig. 4-9.** Size-versus-time graph for the universe. The next cycle, if there is one, could be matter (solid line) or antimatter (dotted line).

Suppose that the time interval from the fiery birth of the universe to its fiery end, if it does indeed end that way, is a circle that is repeated for each cycle. Then events in the next cycle will be an exact repeat of those in this cycle. In fact, you could presume this cycle to be an exact replica of the last one. Not very much the same, not even an almost perfect facsimile, but an *identical copy.*

This makes it possible to have finite time without ever being constrained by a beginning or ending. It is, in a sense, the worst of all possible worlds. The first thought that comes to my mind is that it means we live in a time-warp prison. I am not the first to come up with this theory; apparently it is ages old. There might be some comfort in the fact that if time is indeed circular, then the repeat cycle is still many billions of years off. That's plenty of time for a lot of things to happen.

Cause/effect relationships take on entirely new meaning if you think of time as circular. Then, future events might indeed be causative factors of past ones because the recent past is also the distant future. Cause/effect forces can be illustrated as arrows, or vectors, through the time circle (Fig. 4-10). They might operate over extremely long intervals of time. The result is an immensely large, complicated network of space, time, cause, and effect but it is all fixed in the Grand Scheme of things.

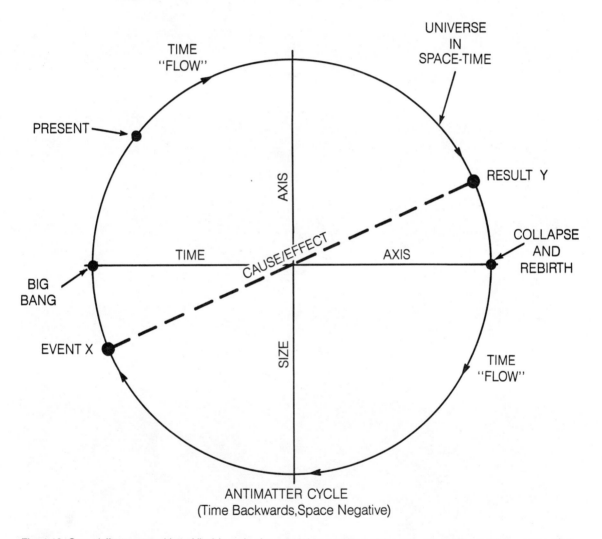

**Fig. 4-10.** Cause/effect vectors (dotted line) in a circular space-time rendition of the universe. In this model, the next cycle is shown as antimatter. Here the next cycle is identical to the cycle previous to the present one; time traverses a circle in which events are identical in each revolution.

Some people shiver at the thought of a universe like that. But many have been searching for exactly this kind of model for reality ever since they have been able to think. If you are disappointed in having arrived at the conclusion you have always wanted, remember something Mr. Spock once said on the famous television series "Star Trek": You might find that the wanting is better than the having; it is illogical but often true.

# CHAPTER 5

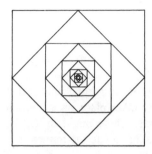

# It's About Time That...

**H**AVE YOU EVER HEARD SOMEONE SAY, "HE'S DUE FOR A HIT" AT A BASEBALL GAME? The guy has gone hitless in 34 consecutive at-bats. It's "about time" he does something. He's batting .250; that means he ought to get a hit once in every four at-bats. The guy is "due." Its 0-and-2. He just has to get a hit. The chances must be very great. But he takes a called strike three down the middle.

Miami hasn't had a severe hurricane since Betsy swiped the area in 1965 (as of this writing). It is true that severe storms do not occur very often anywhere on the earth, and Miami, although among the most susceptible geographical regions in the United States, might get minimal hurricane winds once in seven or eight years from a tropical cyclone. But it's been over 20 years since a real hurricane has pounded the area. Are they "due" there? Is it "about time" for a blow?

Although the actual probability of an event such as a baseball player getting a hit or a hurricane hitting Miami does not change from occasion to occasion, there are other factors involved. Have you ever noticed that things seem to happen in batches? For example, one severe blizzard is followed three days later by another even worse? Or a coin comes up "heads" eleven times in a row even though theoretically you'd have to flip it for days or even weeks to have that be likely? I have noticed this phenomenon and never did think I'd be able to prove it in any other way except through my own actual experience. But now, scientists are unraveling this mystery. It is called "chaos." An excellent book by James Gleick is now available on this subject.*

## Things Happen in Bunches

Our hypothetical baseball player will eventually break his slump. Those who have played any sport know that when this happens, it often takes place dramatically. While the

---

*James Gleick, *Chaos: Making a New Science* (New York: Viking Press, 1987).

player might go hitless in many more at-bats, once he comes out of the slump, he might get six or eight hits in a row and then proceed to go on a rampage that sets a record for consecutive games in which he gets safely on base.

Athletes such as swimmers and runners know that the improvement comes in spurts, with plateaus during which their times might remain the same for long periods. An example is shown in Fig. 5-1 as a graph of the date (by months during a hypothetical year) versus time for the 100-meter freestyle sprint. I can vouch for this phenomenon in competitive swimming (although I never could swim as fast as the hypothetical racer depicted in Fig. 5-1).

Not only is it true that things occur in bunches, but they happen, or are manifested, in bunches of bunches. In fact this takes place on a multiple scale, extending indefinitely down and indefinitely up in size. There might in fact be infinitely many identical, or smaller, recurrent patterns from the tiny to the immense.

This strange phenomenon was first discovered pictorially by an engineer/mathematician with International Business Machines (IBM) named Benoit Mandelbrot. He noticed that similar patterns occurred in such apparently unrelated phenomena as the fluctuations of cotton prices and the distribution of incomes in an economy. His colorful pictorial renditions of patterns as they recur on larger and smaller scales is now almost legendary. It would seem that Mandelbrot has, among other abilities, a flair for making his subject fascinating and beautiful to look at, even if you don't necessarily know what the patterns mean.

Recall the correlation between the sales of television sets in Great Britain since 1945 and the incidence of heart attacks (back in Chapter 2). The two curves followed almost exactly the same ups and downs. You might be tempted to draw conclusions about this that have no real logical foundation; for example, the more televisions sold, the less exercise people got, the more overweight and out-of-shape they became, and the more likely they were to have heart attacks. This might be somewhat true, but it cannot explain the uncanny exactness with which the two curves followed each other. Perhaps they were coincident for a completely unsuspected reason, a fundamental principle so ingrained in the nature of reality that it has been overlooked.

Mandelbrot noticed that patterns tended to recur not only with time, but regardless of scale. Short-term changes in a variable followed more or less exactly the same variations as long-term changes. Traditionally, short-term and long-term changes in, say, the climate, are thought to be unrelated. A single violent hurricane season could be just a coincidence or perhaps the result of an unusual gulf-stream path. But in the longer frame of time, fluctuations might be caused by general global warming, sunspot changes, or even alterations in the radiant energy output of the sun. Mandelbrot noticed that the large-scale and long-range changes were in identical patterns with small-scale and short-term changes. Events occur in bunches; the bunches themselves are prone to take place in similar bunches following the same pattern. And this goes on over and over, both with increasing and decreasing scale. An analogy might be drawn, crudely, by placing geometric forms inside each other so that they always fit in exactly the same relative manner (Fig. 5-2).

What might cause this? How can order result from the apparently random interaction of unrelated phenomena? You would expect that short-term variations would not mean

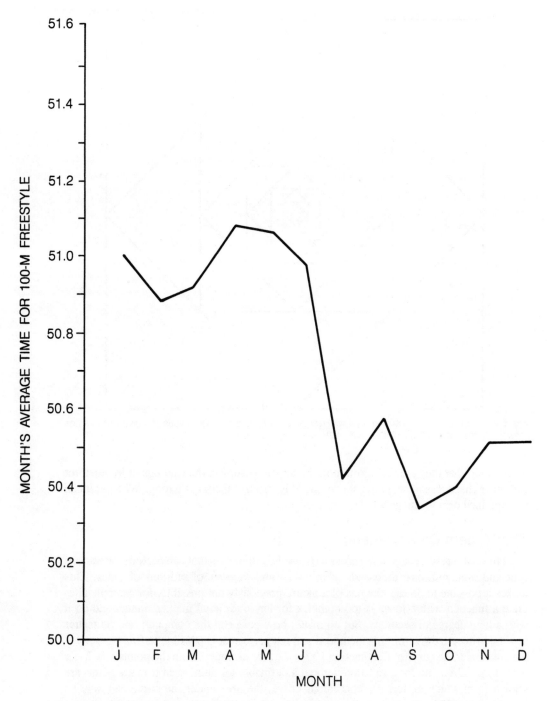

**Fig. 5-1.** Hypothetical times for 100-meter freestyle, averaged over each month of a certain year. Improvement tends to occur in spurts, in this case between June and July.

**Fig. 5-2.** A regular pattern of squares set within squares, *ad infinitum*. The vertices of a given square correspond to the center points of the sides of the next larger square.

much at all, that they are unimportant in the larger sense. But the findings of Mandelbrot and other chaos researchers have shown that this intuitive theory is wrong. Whether it can be explained or not, things are the way they are.

## The Modern Data Gatherer

Nowadays researchers have access to powerful computers that can perform operations over and over, millions, thousands of millions, and millions of millions of times. This makes it possible to do calculations of a nature previously not possible, for example integrate a function with a formula too complex for any traditional mathematician and do it with a high degree of accuracy. But no matter how powerful the computer and no matter how microscopic the error, this method is still not perfect. It is possible to find—exactly— the area under the curve of the function $f(x) = 2x^3$, for example, from the points $x = 2$ to $x = 3$ (Fig. 5-3A). But for a function without a definable formula, even if many points are known from which to derive a continuous curve, the area under the curve can only be approximated. This is done for a hypothetical function $g(x)$ from $x = 2$ to $x = 3$ by breaking the area into many small rectangles, each with height equal to the value of $g(x)$ at the midpoint of the base of each rectangle (Fig. 5-3B).

A tiny error might still be regarded as imperfect, and this is an entirely different sort of reality from the Cartesian perfection familiar to the traditional pure mathematician or the high-school calculus student.

The tendency for a small error (even a tiny error so small that it cannot be detected) to affect large-scale events is called the Butterfly Effect. Can a butterfly taking off in China affect the development, intensity, and ultimate destructive power of a hurricane months later? That butterfly creates a tiny air disturbance that could make the difference between a minor tropical wave and a killer cyclone that ruins hundreds of lives. Or so they say. But is this effect real or just a product of some scientists' vivid imaginations? We can never know for certain whether a given butterfly taking off will have such an effect because things only happen once; we can't go back in time and do things over without the butterfly. Evidence suggests, however, that events do take place in such a manner as to make small things significant.

An example might be if you were to catch a disease. Say you go out biking in the rain and subsequently catch a cold. The cold develops into pneumonia, and you survive by the proverbial skin of your teeth. Might things have turned out differently if the temperature had been one hundredth of a degree warmer, or if one less raindrop had fallen?

Modern data gatherers certainly gather a lot of data. But there is sometimes no way to tell which of these little bits of information are vitally important and which are not. It seems almost as if the more sophisticated our ability to get information becomes, the more difficult it is to make sense out of it all. A computer will never exist that can keep track of the motions of every atom, proton, neutron, electron, quark, or other particle on our planet. If that could somehow be done, it could be possible to predict weather events everywhere in the world for days or weeks in advance solely on the basis of the movements of these particles. If you could log the temperature, humidity, and pressure of every cubic parcel of air measuring one centimeter on an edge over the whole earth, you might be able to determine where they will be in terms of temperature, humidity, and pressure a few seconds or minutes into the future. But in a year? Impossible.

Scientists have been searching for some set of laws that govern all things, and that might allow for precise weather predictions months and years in advance. But for all the computers on the face of this planet put together, the psychics are just about as reliable for long-term weather forecasting as are the meteorologists, at least when it comes to knowing whether it will be raining in Chicago at 3:30 p.m. Central Standard Time on November 20, 2003. The science of chaos insinuates that there is a way to tell, but the amount of data needed to make that prediction is so vast as to outnumber all of the computers that can possibly be made from raw materials on the planet.

## Scale Parallels

In chaos, patterns are repeated in large and small sizes regardless of the physical phenomena involved. A good example is vividly apparent when comparing a photograph of a spiral galaxy with that of a hurricane as seen from space.

This particular example has always fascinated me. Stars are to water droplets as stellar spiral arms are to rain bands. The eye of the hurricane is calm—could this imply that there exists a black hole at the center of every spiral galaxy? The water droplets, carried by

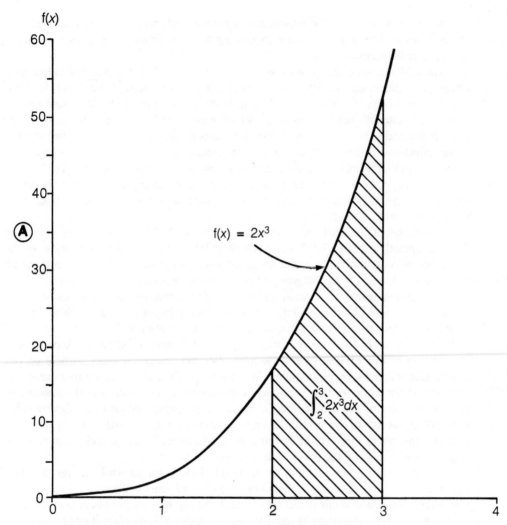

**Fig. 5-3.** At (A), the area under the curve can be figured exactly by means of integral calculus. At (B), approximation is done by means of constructing rectangles under the curve.

winds, spiral inward more and more rapidly as they approach the central core, or *eyewall*, of the hurricane; in the galaxy, the stars move faster and faster as they spiral inward toward the center. A speeded-up picture of a hurricane, compared with the much more time-expanded picture of a galaxy, would produce even more vivid similarities in the behavior of these two different systems.

Air pressure is like gravitation. Both exert force on things. Both produce the same kind of spiral as does the turbulence in a bathtub drain as the water spirals down. There is also the temptation to compare these phenomena with the movements of electrons around the core of an atom or the planets' movement around the sun. These very same spiral eddies are found in the chaotic patterns observed by Benoit Mandelbrot. The Spiral of

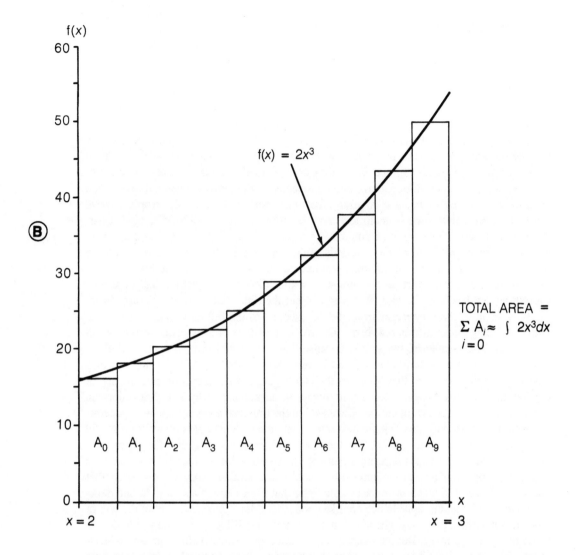

$f(x)$

$f(x) = 2x^3$

TOTAL AREA $=$
$\sum\limits_{i=0} A_i \approx \int 2x^3 dx$

$A_0$  $A_1$  $A_2$  $A_3$  $A_4$  $A_5$  $A_6$  $A_7$  $A_8$  $A_9$

$x$

$x = 2$                    $x = 3$

Archimedes (a standard sort of spiral in analytic geometry) is found in nature in various different places. All of these structural parallels are more than just coincidence—they have to be. But what is behind it all? Why does nature favor the rotating spiral structure on such a vast scale?

Scale parallels are also seen in such events as the slumping of baseball players. During the 1960s, when the Minnesota Twins had Harmon Killebrew and company, it was said that the team was playing well when Killebrew played well, and the team slumped when Killebrew slumped. That may or may not have been true; the team won the pennant in 1965 with Killebrew injured during part of the season. But it is often true that a team rallies when several players get hits in succession. Hits happen in bunches. That's what makes for ten-run innings and 15-2 ball games. They happen a lot. And wins, those results of bunches of hits, come in bunches. So do losses. Recent years have not produced the next-larger-scale occurrence of this phenomenon, the "dynasty." But chances are excellent there will be a "dynasty" team, a powerhouse that wins pennants for years in a row. That is not the exception, but the rule. It's about time for a baseball "dynasty." (I'll be rooting for the Twins.)

Patterns repeat in scales of space and also of time. The time-space of Einstein makes it easy to see why this should be the case. Time can be illustrated as a dimension; you could cut out one spatial dimension and replace it with time to obtain time-space drawings. An example is shown in Fig. 5-4 for a circling airplane. Time is represented here as moving upward along an axis perpendicular to the two space axes that define the plane in which the airplane circles. Similar illustrations can be made for other events. When considering time as a dimension, patterns can be repeated in the four-dimensional time-space continuum. Hurricanes become rotating structures that are born in the tropics, move through the temperate zone (sometimes), and die either from lack of heat or land resistance in most cases. Galaxies are formed by a process not yet fully known, but they rotate and die, perhaps when all of the matter is pulled into the center, or perhaps when the whole universe falls in upon itself some hundreds of billions of years in the future. All of these structures become parts of one single, vast four-dimensional picture that represents everything that has been, is now, and ever will be: the time-space cosmos picture. From the very small to the very large, from the nanosecond to the billion-year eon, there are patterns. Things exist in ordered form, the structure of these forms being similar in all scales—not by coincidence, but simply because this is the way in which reality is built.

It is comforting to think that ordered beings such as people could develop out of a basically chaotic structure. Reality favors the convergence of fragments despite the law of entropy that dictates that disorder should always be increasing. Why is it that order can evolve at all, when the law of entropy dictates that the universe must always be degenerating, and most cosmologists think the universe began in a violent explosion where it would seem everything was up to chance? The temptation arises again to say that God is responsible. Some might even use this as an argument for the existence of God: He exists and He opposes entropy. It is not hard to make other theological parallels, too. You could say that entropy is like evil in that it is an inexorable force that tirelessly strives for cold and darkness, while order and its appearance are like good, that flourishes on account of the will of God. It is not my place to say whether or not I believe that; I'll leave it up to you to decide those things for yourself. But the existence of ordered patterns, arising from an environment where some think it could never possibly happen—that's fascinating. It's about time someone like Benoit Mandelbrot came along and, if not proving the exact cause for it, at least demonstrate that it is more than just our imaginations.

## The Bumpy Ride of Life

How do you put chaos theory to work in your life? Can you derive some benefit out of knowing that order can produce disorder and vice versa?

One example is to find a function that can describe the world population as a function of time. The simplest model allows for an exponential increase in population, but this so-called Malthusian model (named after its inventor, Malthus) does not take into account such limiting factors as the available supply of food, the spread of disease, and of course, natural disasters and wars. The Malthusian model is correct only when the population is well below a certain critical level, where limiting factors begin to level it out.

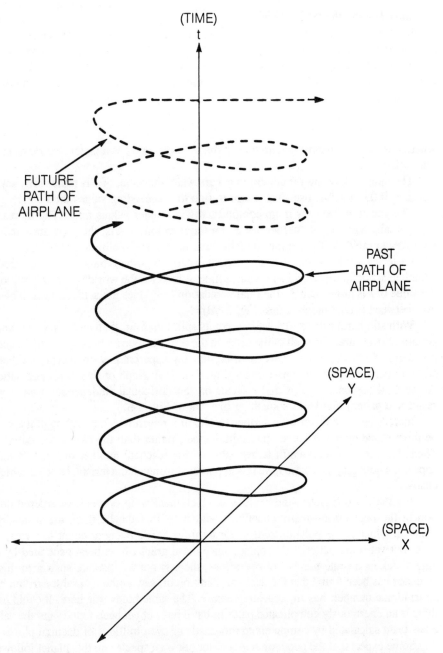

**Fig. 5-4.** Space-time plot, dimensionally reduced, of a circling airplane. The future is depicted as rising vertically. The dotted line shows the future path of the plane, including its final approach.

Interestingly, the leveling-out process is not a smooth one, but a bumpy one. In the simplest case, the population increases and reaches a peak but then falls back as some kind of catastrophe, such as an outbreak of war, occurs. Then the population increases again, and a damped oscillation takes place as the number of people settles to a steady state (Fig. 5-5A). This is easy to envision in the real sense, but its basis can be described purely in mathematical terms. The Malthusian equation for population increase is

$$x_{n+1} = rx_n (1 - x_n)$$

where $n$ is an integer starting with $n = 0$, the initial $x_0$, and $r$ is a factor that represents the rate of increase.

The simple, leveling-off condition occurs when the value of $r$ is rather low, say, 2.5. Let $x_0 = 0.03$. You can use a calculator to find the succeeding values for $x_n$.

The situation becomes more complicated with higher values for $r$. The increasing $r$ value is said to provide a "harder drive" for the iteration; that is, the population increases with greater rapidity. The $r$ value could increase in real life by eliminating birth control, by administering fertility drugs, or—this sounds cruel, but perhaps harsh realism is needed to stimulate action in this world—provide sufficient food for the world's starving millions. If the value of $r$ is large enough, the final population level does not settle, but oscillates forever between two or more values (Fig. 5-5B).

With still harder drive, the settling points split into four, then eight, sixteen, and at a certain critical value for $r$, all of the order in the settling appears to break down. Then, the population fluctuates wildly, never settling into any apparent pattern except that there are certain maximum and minimum limits (Fig. 5-5C). A graph of this, with population on the vertical (dependent) axis and $r$ factor on the horizontal (independent) axis, would result in a pattern that looks something like that of Fig. 5-6.

Increasing the $r$ factor even further results in a return to order, although there might be three stable points or some other odd number, rather than the two in the initial state. Then chaos returns until a still larger value of $r$ is reached; another ordered "window" appears. These graphs always have this apparent shifting characteristic between order and chaos.

Are the chaos regions—the $r$ values at which there is no evidence of ordered fluctuation in the population—really chaotic? Could it be that maybe there are a quadrillion points at which the population settles? Or a million? Too many to count in a reasonable time, but yet some pattern? Of course, since these graphs have been generated by computers making a finite number of operations, there is not an absolute answer to this. No evidence has been found that the decimal rendition of, say, $e$ (the natural logarithm base), an irrational number, has any repeating nature. The same holds true here. It could be that there is an enormously complicated pattern, but it has not yet been found, and the value of $e$ has been calculated by computers to thousands or even millions of decimal places.

Some expect that the population model for our own species on this planet follows this rule. Whether the driving force, or $r$ value, is sufficiently high so as to produce a chaotic (non-patterned) fluctuation once the breaking point is reached is not yet known. That point hasn't been reached yet, but it will. It's only a matter of time. Some say it's about time that happened, that the breaking point is going to come soon. These people point to the AIDS epidemic or the turmoil in the Middle East as evidence. There have been such doomsayers ever since Mount Vesuvius went crazy and obliterated Pompeii, that ancient city with its

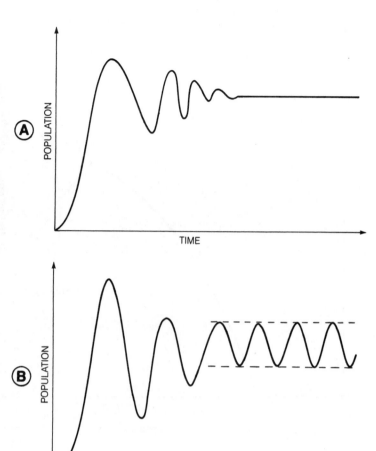

**Fig. 5-5.** Population-versus-time curves for various values of the *r* factor. At (A), small *r* factor results in eventual stability. At (B), a larger *r* factor produces an oscillating final population. At (C), a still larger *r* factor gives rise to a final population that fluctuates chaotically between two extremes.

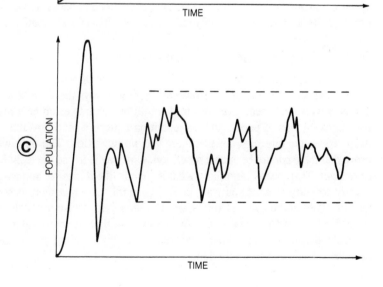

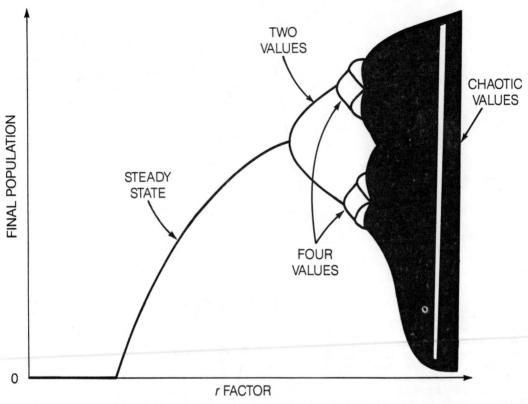

**Fig. 5-6.** Curve of final population as a function of *r* factor.

"sinful" population. The theory of chaos dictates that such a point will be reached, not because humans are immoral or because of some cosmic battle between the devil and the Lord, but because reality is simply made that way. It's a purely mathematical inevitability.

## True Order and True Randomness

It is difficult to say whether there is some pattern of repetition in a sequence of numbers that appears to have none. However, there is always the uncertainty whether enough numbers were evaluated. Even if it took a million years to examine a printout of consecutive digits on tons of paper, and no repetition pattern was discovered, that wouldn't, by itself, constitute logical proof that there was no repetition. The only way to do that is to prove that there *cannot* be such a repetition. One way is to use the technique of *reductio ad absurdum*. That means essentially what it sounds like it means. You assume a proposition exactly contrary to what you want to prove—in this case that there is some repeating pattern of digits in the decimal rendition of *e*—and then derive a conclusion that is impossible. Such a conclusion takes the form A & $-$A, that is, some statement (A) along with its exact negation ($-$A). Then you know that the original proposition must be false because it leads to a contradiction.

Mathematical proofs are examples of what might be called pure order. Some simple mathematical universes are perfect in the sense that they consist of statements whose truth value (either true or false) can always be found in a finite number of steps by proof, based on a set of axioms and definitions and logical rules of procedure. The mathematician G. H. Hardy was especially fond of pointing this out: mathematics is a "perfect" science. It was up to the logicians, Kurt Godel in particular, to throw a monkey wrench into this machinery of complacency by proving his famous Incompleteness Theorem. In this theorem, the conclusion is truly bizarre: For first-order logic systems, there are statements whose truth value *cannot* be determined using a finite number of steps. This results in a situation that is annoyingly imperfect but not yet perfectly imperfect. It is partly chaotic but not completely. It is something like the graph of Fig. 5-6—there is order (the statements that can either be proved or disproved) and chaos (those statements that cannot be proved or disproved) in a mixture.

Is there such a thing as perfect order and perfect disorder in the universe? Entropy is another example. The universe, according to some scientists, was once very hot and dense. Unimaginably so. But did it have an infinite temperature, and was it confined to a geometric point with dimensional span zero, zero, zero? That would be the ultimate state of order. The order would be so absolute that there would be no measurements of any kind possible. It is unknown if this was ever the case, but most scientists doubt it. Very hot, yes; very small, yes. But not an infinitely hot bundle of everything noplace. The universe will, if it does not recollapse, gradually cool down and attain a very low, uniform temperature. But will it ever expand so that it has zero density and no heat at all? That would require an infinite amount of time. A temperature-versus-time graph of a theoretically perfect universe, evolving from total order to total disorder over an infinite amount of time, might look like the illustration of the function $f(x) = 1/x$, shown in Fig. 5-7A. The volume-versus-time graph might look like the function $g(x) = \sqrt{x}$, as in Fig. 5-7B.

Perfect order and perfect disorder might happen in the world of pure mathematics, but even then only when there are severe restrictions. In actual reality, you might wonder if true order or true randomness exist at all. Random-number lists are generally prepared from algorithms that produce the appearance of a sequence of nonterminating, nonrepeating digits. But the very fact that such a generating algorithm exists seems to make the resulting list of digits nonrandom. A good test would be to see whether the same result occurs when the algorithm is executed over and over. There might be a choice of several "starting" digits, say 0 through 9 or even 000 through 999, creating possibilities in powers of 10; still, the results would be predictable after that digit was chosen. A truly random sequence of digits would be unpredictable from any point onward. There might in fact be no such thing. A die will fall in a way that can be predicted if the components of its initial motion, the nature of the surface on which it will land, the character of the air currents in the vicinity of the die, and so on are all known. Even individual molecules can be followed and their future paths predicted if the parameters are definable with sufficient accuracy. Perfect accuracy is not needed. We may not yet have the technology to forecast, for example, where a given molecule of $H_2O$ will be 24 years, 3 days, and 11 hours (to the nearest trillionth of a second) from the moment you read this comma, but in theory, we *could* have it. Or so it would seem.

The search for perfect order is as old as science, even as old as thought. It probably stems from the need for a deity, and many perceive such a being as perfect—part of the

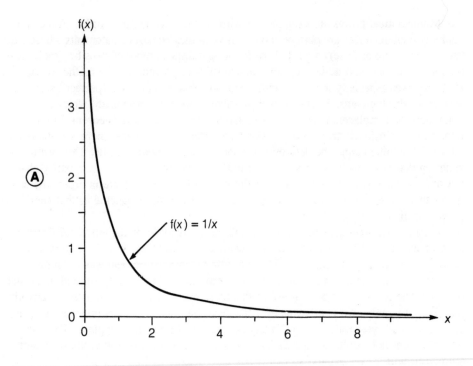

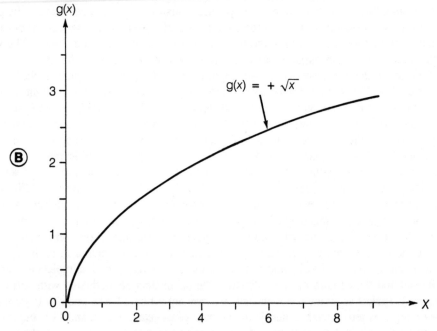

**Fig. 5-7.** At (A), the temperature-versus-time curve for the universe might resemble the function $f(x) = 1/x$. At (B), the curve of volume versus time probably resembles that of the function $g(x) = +\sqrt{x}$, assuming the universe does not have sufficient mass to cause eventual collapse.

definition of its existence. A search for total disorder or total randomness results in the discovery that chaos is everywhere in reality. But is there perfect disorder any more than there is perfect order? It seems that both ends of this spectrum, of this continuum, represent their own kind of perfection. In the experimentalist's world where error is always present, neither perfection nor randomness become total. It is up to the theorist to ponder this question. Since "one experimentalist can keep a dozen theorists busy," it appears that there is no lack of material to serve as fodder for the theoretician's brainstorms. Perhaps the title "Professor of Chaos" will appear on someone's door at some university in the not-too-distant future, and it will be there in all seriousness. Such a person would not have lack of things to do.

# CHAPTER 6

# Connections to the Other Side

ALL OF THE PHENOMENA ASSOCIATED WITH EXTRASENSORY PERCEPTION (ESP) AND THE occult are rather nonscientific, aren't they? That sort of thing is avoided by the scientific community as much as possible. I am not sure why this seems to be the case, but it is almost as if scientists have something against the very notion that such business might even hold some grain of truth.

Yet we used to hear stories that our former own President Reagan read his horoscope. Well, so do I sometimes. One day the horoscope told me I ought to watch my diet and exercise. That happened to be a day I had decided to be a "couch potato" and eat like crazy, and I wasn't about to let some horoscope tell me that I had to "diet and exercise." But in a sense, I was following an essential ingredient of any sound diet-exercise program: I was taking a day off. In fact, I maintain a diet and exercise program as rigorous as any person in this country with the exception of serious amateur or professional athletes, and rest is a part of any serious program. Thus I did in fact follow my horoscope that day. But its advice didn't influence my decisions. Horoscopes are just fun to read. They give our minds time off from the serious, humdrum routine, even if they have no basis in reality. What humorless robot should have anything against the President taking a little mental rest now and then, too?

But there is a very real danger in taking horoscopes, or any other of the ESP/occult things, too seriously. This danger is not the possibility that a person in power might push a red button and blow up the world. It is a possibility for anyone who gets involved with these phenomena (or the lack of them, some may insist). These particular fields of endeavor have a way of becoming mind-consuming. It is easy to get obsessed with them. Then they cause real trouble. This is especially true of the occult. There may be no devil, witches, or sorcerers; however, if you make them up in your mind with sufficient effort, the ideas themselves can become quite deleterious to your thinking. This, at the very least, ought to serve as a warning for those interested in such phenomena.

# ESP and Emotions

Experiments have been conducted for ESP, especially for telepathy, or the ability of one person to send messages via thought energy to another person. Numbered cards, colored marbles, and various other techniques have been used. Generally many tests are done, and the number of correct responses is then compared with the chances in pure guesswork. For example, if there are 13 cards (ace through king counting as 1 through 13), then there should be correct guesses in exactly $1/13$ of the cases. For 1300 guesses, 100 of them would, on average, be correct—if they were in fact pure guesses. Such experiments have resulted in about the same number of correct responses as if they were guesses. Once in a while there is a significantly higher percentage of correctness; occasionally there are far fewer. However, there has never been a consistent showing of evidence in favor of someone having telepathic powers. A good indicator of this is the fact that there has never been such a person employed by the President. Never has the job of "telepather" been filled on any trip to the Kremlin. Despite what might be in the tabloids, hard evidence has been elusive.

Another method of transmitting and receiving messages involves color, such as those of the spectrum: red, orange, yellow, green, blue, indigo, and violet. Again, as with numbers, the conclusive evidence has been lacking. Still other methods involve scenes shown on screens with slide projectors. I can remember doing ESP experiments with a friend when I was in high school. I was the sender and he was the receiver. Colored marbles were used and he seemed to get a large percentage of the colors correct—far more than what would be dictated by sheer probability. Then I showed family slides from past years on a screen that he could not see. He was lying on a couch in the darkened room and could not see me or any reflection of the image on the screen. A photograph of the lake in summer, complete with boats—with our boat in the middle—came up. He guessed it to almost every last detail. Then a slide of autumn leaves, brightly colored, with the low-angle slanting sun and long shadows, came on. I have always disliked autumn—it is invariably followed by winter! I felt a rush of "the fun is over" feeling. He said he could feel the fall. It was amazing. There were no scientists present so the experiment must be considered unscientific. But I won't forget it.

How often has the emotion factor been considered in scientific tests of the phenomenon of telepathy or other ESP tests? You are probably familiar with instances where someone "had a feeling" and it was later found that some dramatic event had occurred at, or nearly at, that moment. Perhaps it was somewhere far away, but it was usually related to some loved one or friend. For example, a man might have a vision that his wife has had a terrible accident, and 1,500 miles away, the event actually happens right then. Occurrences such as these do not happen under controlled laboratory conditions but in real life. The actual universe is not the sterile scientific place that some of us might like it to be, but a turbulent and often unexplainable place.

I believe that ESP might be more of an emotional phenomenon than an intellectual one. If this is true, then the sending of thought messages can be enhanced if the sender and receiver are emotionally involved. Hence, this might not be helpful for those who have dreamed of using ESP for espionage. Sending "dry" information has not generally yielded results that have been significantly better than pure guesswork.

## Clairvoyance

Information can be detected, some have claimed, even if there is no sending person. This is called *clairvoyance*. Examples are the detection of events in the future, events not witnessed by any person, or events that happen among people that the receiver does not know. The ability to predict the future is partly based on knowledge of the facts at present and on scientific principles. If the barometer is falling rapidly, the wind is from the south, it is hot and muggy, and the weather depiction shows an intense cold front approaching, you could conclude that a severe thunderstorm will be hitting. But this might not necessarily take place. It is just very likely, based on past experience. You might get a better idea from the local weather radar information; it shows exactly where the thunderstorms are and in what direction they are moving. On some hot, muggy days, thunderstorms occur, and on other days with exactly the same type of weather, they do not. In the past, before radio communication or even telephones, intuition was often the only way to determine whether a given day would produce severe storms or not. I recall when I was a child it seemed that I had a good sense of this particular weather. I could often tell in the morning that there was likely to be a severe storm, or even a tornado sighting, late in the day. I was correct more often than might be thought purely on the basis of intuition. Could I have been clairvoyant about the short-term weather future?

I apparently still have some of this sense because I predicted the drought of 1988 during the late winter, before there was any evidence of its having begun. I am writing this at the end of June, 1988, and here in southeast Minnesota, the annual precipitation deficit is about 3.5 inches for 1988 so far. My feeling is that the drought will ease in September or October. Thus, I am willing to go out on a limb about this; by the time this book is in print, I will have been proven either right or wrong. (I have been dead wrong before, too, so if I am clairvoyant about the weather, it is a phenomenon that does not always occur.)

Clairvoyance would be thought less frequent or likely than telepathy because it is basically the same thing but with no "sender" except the cosmos. You might think the truth all by itself is less powerful than the truth as thought by a living being. There can be no "brain waves" with the occurrence of clairvoyance unless you imagine that some cosmic mind knows all that is, was, and ever shall be and that people can sense these thoughts. If that is true, then clairvoyance might be more likely than mental telepathy.

There are those who claim to be able to predict the future and their predictions are often made public in tabloids. It would appear that sensationalism is the main motivation for this. Such predictions are often wrong, usually extreme in their nature, and one might doubt if the claimed predictors are really behind what they say or whether their names are being used by someone for the purpose of making money.

## Horoscopes

Astrology is the belief that the stars and planets can be used to tell the future and that their motions actually govern events on Earth. Daily horoscopes are printed in many newspapers, and they usually contain advice, such as "Be tolerant of a loved one's complaints." My favorite horoscope was a joke by a radio announcer on a Minneapolis radio station back in the 1960s: "Today is not a good day to drive a golf ball in a tile bathroom."

The idea that the movements of celestial bodies might influence events on Earth is not as farfetched as might be thought at first. The sun and moon cause tides, and some evidence suggests that similar gravitational effects on human cells might account for certain behavorial changes. The weather can be influenced by the phase of the moon; high tides can cause floods if the moon is new or full. Sunspots affect radio wave propagation. There are possibly some interplanetary effects that we do not yet know exist that can have a profound effect on what happens on our planet.

Astrology takes all this and refines it to a science *so* exact that it makes some skeptical. Your own particular horoscope depends not only on your astrological sign but on the day you were born and even on the hour and minute of your birth. From this, it is said, your entire life story is derived, because the stars and planets were in a certain position then and that is sufficient information, if known, to foretell your whole life. The astrologer bases such information on what is likely to happen; there are certain times when it might be good to consider marriage, for example, and certain times when such a move would best be avoided. How do astrologers get their information? Presumably on past experience. Nonetheless, it is not possible to have gained enough practical experience concerning the effects to make a true astrological science unless billions of people's lives had been analyzed in detail. No one has done such a thing. Coincidences of the past are the only foundation on which astrology can be built, and such coincidences are not necessarily indicative of any special astronomical cause/effect event.

Horoscopes can, however, be self-fulfilling in some cases. If you warned everyone to prepare for a possible outbreak of measles by getting their shots, you might fulfill the prophecy of a horoscope that says a great pestilence will be averted. Or so we might think, but we can never go back in time and find out if the effort produced any beneficial results.

There are historical examples of national leaders who have acted on the advice of their horoscopes. Probably the best-known of these is Adolf Hitler. This has destroyed faith in horoscopes quite effectively. It has also reinforced the notion that astrology is somehow associated with cosmic evil. Many people have the idea that engaging in astrology is akin to tampering with wicked forces. They could have some correctness in this idea, for it seems that whenever people allow themselves to be governed by inanimate things, they are looking for trouble.

I recall an experience in which I was visiting the home of a girl friend in Florida, and her mother was a horoscope enthusiast. She was in fact a student of astrology and offered to give me some detailed information about my life. It was only necessary that I tell her the date of my birth and the time of day I was born. I let her know that I was not certain of the exact time but that it was around 7:00 a.m. Here is a problem. It might have been 6:00 and it might have been 8:00. I'm pretty sure it was early in the morning, but if I am off by an hour, the effects many years afterward might be very significant. A small error would introduce progressively larger and larger uncertainty the farther ahead in time we get. This is a common effect in science. An error of one minute of arc ($1/60$ of an angular degree) when aiming a rifle might not seem like much, and will in fact not be for a nearby target (Fig. 6-1A); but for a very distant target (Fig. 6-1B) the error will be large. I would therefore have to know, to the minute, the time of my birth if I wanted to know what would happen to me when I was 78 years old, for example.

The more serious error was that the lady never asked me which time zone I was born in. This might make up to 12 hours of difference and could even affect the day on which I was born, depending on the point of reference she used. Perhaps the time zone does not matter, although I would think that if the stars were so critical as to make it necessary to

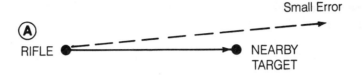

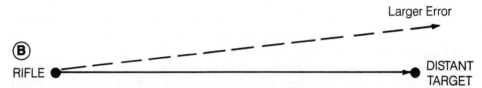

Fig. 6-1. At (A), a small error occurs over a short distance when a rifle is fired at a target. At (B), the greater distance results in a larger error.

specify the exact hour of birth, time zones could not be ignored. That little bit of carelessness shot a big hole in my faith in her ability to predict my future life.

## Astral Projection

This term sounds almost scientific. It is the parapsychologist's and metaphysician's lingo for leaving one's body.

According to most occult people, we all possess a physical body and an astral body. These normally reside in the same place, but the astral body is invisible to human eyes. It can only be seen when we are in the "astral plane." Then the astral body may leave the physical body and travel around, seeing and hearing what goes on in places quite far removed from the physical body. During these times, the physical body is asleep but is still alive, connected to the astral body by a long "umbilical cord" that keeps the person from dying. Should this cord be severed, the person dies; or, if the person dies, the cord disappears and the astral body is presumably left on its own.

Those who claim to have had astral-projection, or out-of-body, experiences report that they can see and hear but not feel, smell or taste, and that they can pass through material objects as if they were ghosts. It is possible, they say, to "will" one's astral body over great distances. Whatever happens in the vicinity of the physical body has no effect on perceptions while in this state. Apparently, any attempt to awaken the physical body during such an out-of-body experience would not work; the body would seem as if it were in a coma, with greatly depressed breathing and heartbeat and unresponsiveness.

Controlled experiments in astral projection have not been done. At least, I have not yet read about this phenomenon in the newspapers as having been verified by scientists at Harvard. It is another of those things that suffers the disadvantage of being incredible—verification of it would cast doubt on the credibility of any scientist. It is just too strange and too charged with sensational overtones.

Suppose that such out-of-body experiences are actually possible and that there is a physical and biological explanation for them. This is not really so terribly hard to imagine. There might well be some concrete part of the consciousness that can be removed from the body by considerable distances. Then you would have, at your immediate disposal, an invaluable tool for interplanetary, interstellar and intergalactic travel, at least insofar as you would be able to go to Jupiter, for example, and see what the place looks like. Out-of-body travel would also be useful in espionage, and the Russians have been accused of (that is, they are evidently involved with) experimenting in this vein.

Astral projection provides an excellent example of why I believe extrasensory perception and occult-related practices are potentially dangerous. I speak from experience. One can become obsessed with such things, and this obsession can be detrimental to a normal, healthy life. Even if there are no "evil forces" and no real astral body, these ideas can take over in the mind and lead one away from productivity, usefulness and happiness. In that way even the ghosts of their ideas can be damaging.

When I was in high school I read a book about ESP and was especially fascinated by the phenomenon of astral projection. I imagined it as a means to see what other planets looked like. I imagined I might be able to travel through four-dimensional time-space or even through more dimensions than four, short-circuiting the relativistic limitations on how far one can travel in a given amount of time. There would be no need to carry any oxygen or food, and the whole business would not cost a penny. Getting others to believe me, should I be successful in my ventures, would have to come with time, once I had perfected the art of out-of-body travel so that I could do it on a moment's notice. I imagined myself sitting in a chair and being able to get right out of my body on cue, making certain to place sufficient padding on the floor underneath my body so that it would not be injured as it slumped into a state of suspended animation, the eyes rolling back and the tongue lolling out, saliva drooling . . . well, I have a vivid imagination. It wasn't long before this conscious train of thought invaded my subconscious and I had my first astral "experience."

If there is such a thing as astral projection, I am quite convinced that this first episode was genuine. I am by no means a believer in the phenomenon, and after having dealt with the way it affected my thinking, I honestly have to say that I really don't care very much whether such things are possible or not. I simply cannot afford to spend that much time thinking about it and certainly have no desire to do any more fiddling around trying to do it.

I was lying on my back in bed and came to realize that I was asleep. It is possible for the mind to wake up while the body remains asleep. Some people have this happen often and it bothers them so much that they occasionally seek the help of psychologists or psychiastrists. I realized that this was the perfect type of condition for me to try to "leave my body." Thus I attempted to make my astral body "sit up" in the bed.

The astral body has been described as having the same form as the physical body, but no mass. The exact nature of it has not been described by those who claim to have had out-of-body experiences (or by anyone else, either). When I tried to sit up in the bed, I felt the motion of sitting up and then went flying all the way across the room, coming to rest belly-down a few feet in front of the closed door. I imagine that had I been asleep and dreaming normally, the rush of excitement I felt at that time would have caused me to waken. But I remained hovering in this prone position, or perhaps I ought to say that my astral body remained there, as if it were floating in a pool of water. The room was too dark to see anything except the shadows of the furniture, but everything looked normal.

Having been given to understand that, in the astral state, one could "will" the astral body through objects such as doors, I "willed" myself to be in the hallway on the other side of the door. It was impossible to open the door and go out in the normal way, because material objects cannot be affected by astral bodies. When I "willed" this to happen, I found myself after a second or two standing in the hallway. Again everything looked normal. The hall light was on, as usual. The bathroom door was ajar a little bit.

I wish, in retrospect, I had had more patience and stayed in this "astral" condition longer. As it was, I "willed" that I be back in my body. Then I awakened normally.

I cannot now say whether this experience was a dream, or whether it was something more. I wrote to the author of the book on ESP that had gotten me interested in astral projection, told him of the experience, and waited for a reply. He wrote back in his own handwriting, telling me that I had indeed had an astral experience and that I could find out more by reading his book entitled such-and-such. My mother had told me that was probably what he would say; he wanted to sell books. His interest in my astral projection, or imagined astral experience, might be genuine and might not, but money was the bottom line. How many 17-year-old boys listen to their mothers?

My experiments with astral projection continued, but never again did I have an experience as vivid as that first one, and never was there any event that suggested I had not been dreaming it all. In fact, some of the experiences were very much like dreams and I must conclude that that is what they really were. I did perceive an increase in heart rate while trying to "leave my body." It seemed also that my blood pressure might have gone up. In this sense it was physically uncomfortable, and I began to suspect it could be dangerous.

But the real danger was my increasing obsession with the whole business. It was starting to take up time that ought to be used for more down-to-earth pursuits in the life of a high-school boy. The swim team was much better for socializing than thinking about the astral plane. One book suggested that in order to facilitate astral projection, it was advisable to neglect your health until you were actually almost ill. That would, the book seemed to say, weaken the bond between the physical and astral bodies and make separation easier. At this point I decided to give up. I wanted to make the state championships in swimming and getting sick on purpose didn't jive with that. Besides, it started to seem stupid and just plain unhealthy, both physically and mentally. My view became, and remains to this day, thus: everyone dies sooner or later, and then there probably won't be any choice but to be in this astral state, so I'll wait until then and get on with life now.

That is good advice for anyone who finds himself or herself getting caught up in astral projection or any other metaphysical business. Such phenomena are interesting, and are worthy, for that reason, of study. But don't go too far because astral projection seems especially likely to cause an unhealthy obsession.

## The Spirit World

At this point, consider speculating on the possible existence of disembodied spirits. Is it possible that there is such a universe, a spiritual plane, perhaps inhabited by astral bodies? If they do exist and do not interact with the "real" universe, there is no way to know whether they exist or not, except to depend on the testimony of those who claim to have left their bodies and been there.

The problem with such claims is that they are often made simply in order to get attention, or even worse, to create a sensation for the purpose of making money. Some people apparently do believe they have interacted with the "spirit world" in some way or other. The most commonly reported phenomena are ghost sightings or witnessing their effects. The effects include such things as temperature changes (usually chills) and psychokinesis. Occasionally, things are moved considerable distances.

I recall an experience while I lived in the Florida Keys that was explained, casually, by the natives as the sort of thing that might be done by a pirate ghost. I was getting ready to leave for a trip and had to shut off the water supply. I made a sign to remind the pool maintenance man that if he turned the water on when cleaning or refilling the pool to shut it off again before he left. I put the sign by the faucets in the little shack where the water apparatus was but didn't turn off the water right then because I had some other things to do before I left and might want a last drink of water. When I got back upstairs and tried to get a glass of water, there was no water pressure. Upon checking down at the water faucets, I found that the water had been shut off. Absentmindedness? I don't think so. I figured it was someone checking the house, perhaps thinking that I had already left. The natives explained that hurricanes in centuries past had been responsible for many shipwrecks in that part of Florida, and it was probably some playful pirate's ghost who shut the water off.

Some people claim to have communicated with ghosts. This is done by means of such practices as seances. In a seance, a group of people sit around a room that is lit by candles or is totally dark. Then mysterious-sounding incantations are recited. Everyone is placed into a situation where small sensory stimuli can be greatly amplified. The shadow of a curtain blowing in a puff of wind or the sound of a bird flying by could be regarded as some supernatural effect, and the expectation of such things puts everyone on edge. It is no wonder that some people claim to have heard voices or seen people long since dead under these conditions. The whole business is deliberately designed to place people under mental and/or emotional stress. If there actually are ghosts, I wonder what they must think of such behavior?

When it comes to spirits and the "afterworld," each person has a unique set of beliefs. Most people don't give it enough thought to delve into such details as whether or not ghosts can make themselves visible, or cause psychokinetic phenomena, or pass through walls, or travel great distances unaffected by the constraints of relativistic time dilation. These questions are unanswered for the moment, but it might be possible to find out some of the answers by means of a methodical scientific inquiry. It would have to be a new kind of science, however, that would take emotional issues into account. These factors, while not seeming "scientific" or subject to analysis, are very real. The world is not sterile of these things, no matter how you may wish it were, and some scientific studies must take emotional factors into consideration. Psychology is one; parapsychology is another.

## Dimensional Constraints

When speaking of "the other side," I refer to any universe that extends beyond or is not a part of our own. Many think of the universe as everything that exists, and it seems at first thought rather meaningless to speak of anything else. How can there be anything besides everything? Yet in the complexity of the whole cosmos, this might well be worth thinking about.

One variable that is often considered as a dimension is time. If time is a dimension in which free travel is possible, this opens up a vast new cosmos. Ghosts could have the power to travel in time, either forward, which can be relativistically possible even for material beings, or backward. Could it be that the real cosmos is seething with spirit beings from all times—past, present and future? We have no way of knowing without communicating with them, and the only way to do that is by means of the methods on which are cast such doubt.

Let us depart from the discussion of spirit beings and psychokinetics, and consider the possibilities for universes other than the one we now have physical contact with.

The number of dimensions could vary from one on upward in integral numbers. A zero-dimensional spatial universe would be a geometric point, a singularity—and while some scientists believe that gravitational collapse could create such universes, nothing can go on in such a place and therefore its existence is not of useful consequence.

A one-dimensional universe would take the form of a line or linear curve. Such a universe might be unbounded, in the form of a straight line or infinitely long curve. Or, it could take the form of a line segment. A finite-but-unbounded one-dimensional universe might exist in the form of a closed curve. These three possibilities are illustrated, with two examples of each, in Figs. 6-2, 6-3 and 6-4.

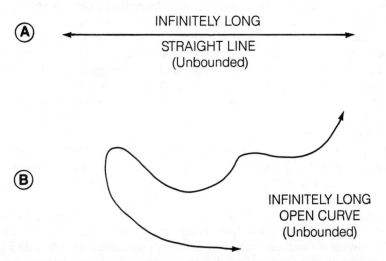

Fig. 6-2. One-dimensional universes. At (A), an infinitely long, straight line. At (B), an infinitely long, non-Euclidean line.

In a one-dimensional universe, it would be possible to imprison a being by means of just two points, one point on each side of that being. A being in a one-dimensional cosmos would see only a point as the field of view. Perhaps if it was always foggy, the being could tell how far away an object was. It would not be possible to see anything past an object in such a universe because there could be no depth perception. It would be, by our standards, a terribly dull place. Yet, such universes could exist. They would have no mass and no

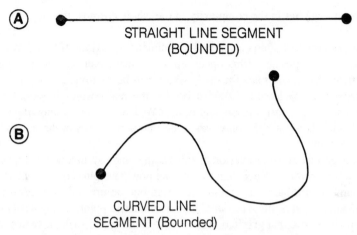

STRAIGHT LINE SEGMENT
(BOUNDED)

CURVED LINE
SEGMENT (Bounded)

**Fig. 6-3.** Finite one-dimensional universes. At (A), a straight line segment; at (B), a curved line segment.

spatial breadth or height to us, and there would thus be no means by which we could detect them. Mathematically, they might exist, but for practical purposes such as communicating with residents there, such universes might as well not exist.

Perhaps you have read about "Flatland," a hypothetical plane universe of two dimensions. Such a universe is infinitely more accommodating than a one-dimensional cosmos. It is easy to imagine how movement could occur on the surface of, say, a sheet of paper. Such a universe would be infinitely thin but could extend forever in one or both of its planar dimensions. An unbounded two-dimensional universe might be flat, or Euclidean, so that the familiar laws of plane geometry would hold. Or, it might take the form of a paraboloid or other non-Euclidean but infinite surface (Fig. 6-5). A two-dimensional universe could be finite in one dimension and infinite in the other; an example of this is an infinitely long cylinder (Fig. 6-6). In this two-dimensional continuum, one dimension is unbounded but finite and the other is infinite. Depending on the direction of travel, if you were to circumnavigate this universe, you might end up going on forever. Of course, there are infinitely many variations on this theme. Finally, a two-dimensional universe might be closed in both dimensions (Fig. 6-7). The example shown is of a sphere, but an ellipsoid, cube, or any other closed surface also has this closed property.

We could not communicate with beings in such a universe nor even tell, by any physical means we know of, that it was there. Beings in "Flatland" could not tell of the existence of a universe not identical with theirs unless by coincidence a patch of their universe exactly overlapped with a patch of another having the same number of dimensions.

Some might be wondering, "What's the point in even discussing such universes if there is no way to prove or disprove that they exist?" The answer, besides the simple response that it is a mathematical game and mathematical games can be fun, lies in the fact that we might someday be able to bridge the dimension gap. It seems impossible now, but going faster than about 25 miles per hour was once thought dangerous because it might scramble people's brains and make them into idiots. This was less than two centuries ago. Perhaps in another two centuries, that "Flatland" slanting through your room at this very moment might be detectable, and we just might be able to communicate with the beings of that continuum.

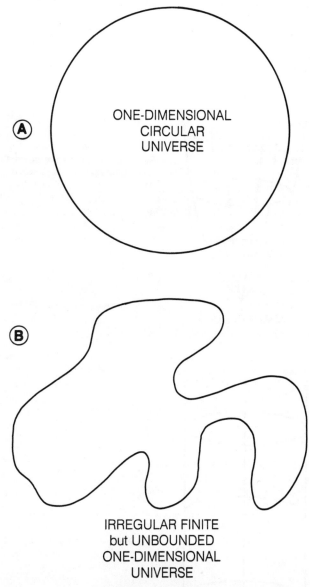

ONE-DIMENSIONAL
CIRCULAR
UNIVERSE

Ⓐ

Ⓑ

IRREGULAR FINITE
but UNBOUNDED
ONE-DIMENSIONAL
UNIVERSE

**Fig. 6-4.** Finite, but unbounded, one-dimensional universes. At (A), a circle; at (B), an irregular shape.

## More than Three Dimensions

According to the well-known physicist Stephen Hawking, there might be other universes besides the one we perceive as having three spatial dimensions. Hawking speaks of millions upon millions of universes having evolved like a vast foam of space-time in which individual constituents could have up to eleven dimensions. Imagining things in a universe of four spatial dimensions is impossible for us unless we employ the crutch of mathematics.

**Fig. 6-5.** A two-dimensional paraboloidal universe. This universe is infinite.

PARABOLOID
(Two-Dimensional)

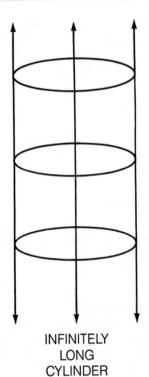

**Fig. 6-6.** An infinitely long cylindrical universe.

INFINITELY
LONG
CYLINDER

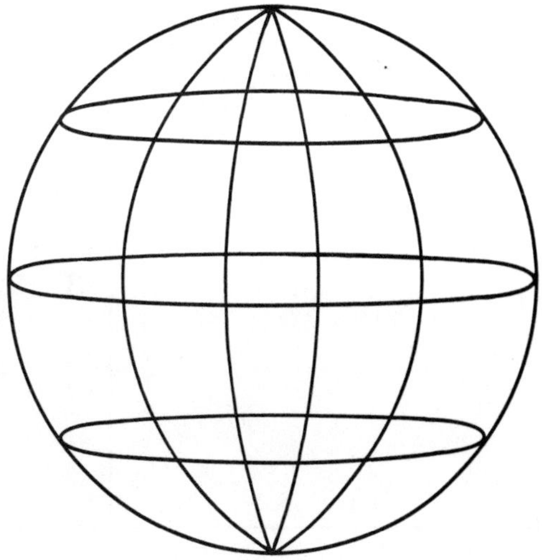

**Fig. 6-7.** A spherical universe. Many scientists believe that our cosmos is shaped like this but in one added dimension.

SPHERE

Assume the four-dimensional universe exists. Those four-dimensional dummies can't even tell that our universe slants through *their* room at this instant. Despite their dimensional superiority, they seem to be quite stupid compared with us. They haven't even tried to envision our restricted habitat and haven't attempted communication with us for at least a few hundred million years Earth time.

In an *n*-dimensional universe (where *n* is a positive integer—$n = 1, 2, 3, \ldots$), exactly *n* coordinates are needed to uniquely define the position of a point. In two dimensions, this is the familiar Cartesian plane (Fig. 6-8), with coordinates *x* and *y* on two axes beginning at an origin $(x, y) = (0,0)$. On a spherical surface, latitude and longitude can be used. For three dimensions, add the *z* axis to the Cartesian system (Fig. 6-9), or distance from the center of a sphere, to these. It is always true that *n* numbers are needed in *n* dimensions. Fewer than *n* coordinate values will not specify the position for at least some points; more than *n* coordinate values will cause redundancies that are avoidable by using fewer values. In this sense, a time coordinate *t* can be added to any *n*-dimensional spatial universe, making it an $n + 1$-dimensional universe. However, it is not possible yet to move about as freely in time as in space.

Could it be that there are universes with hundreds or even infinitely many spatial dimensions? In a universe having infinitely many dimensions, it would take an infinite time to specify the coordinates of a point because there would be infinitely many values! For example, say the coordinates are $n_1, n_2, n_3, \ldots$ and that a point P was given by the coordinates in the ordered infinituple $(n_1, n_2, n_3, \ldots)$. The problem is that you could never finish writing the ordered infinituple, and there would thus be an infinite ambiguity as to exactly where the point was. Not a very good state of affairs. However, mathematically, the point might exist. For a point such as is given by the numeric digits of the square root of 2 would give $n_1 = 1, n_2 = 4, n_3 = 1, n_4 = 4, n_5 = 2$, and so on because the square root of 2 is given by 1.4142 to five significant digits. The actual value is an infinitely long sequence of decimal digits, but they all exist, even if they can never be written down in a finite list.

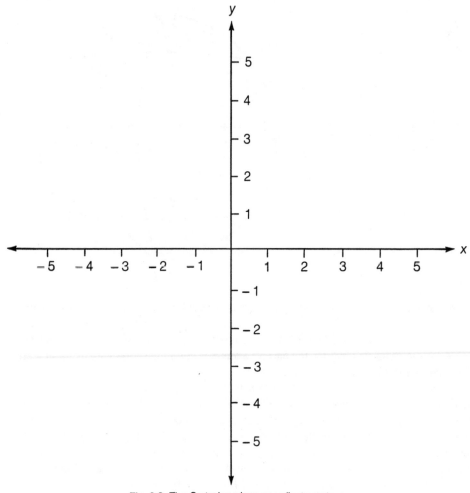

**Fig. 6-8.** The Cartesian plane coordinate system.

How would we communicate with universes having more or fewer dimensions than ours? If our universe is mathematically zero in thickness with respect to the next higher-dimensioned ones, and if two-dimensional universes have zero thickness to us, then perhaps there is no way to communicate. But space and time might be quantized so that our universe has some measurable (if tiny) thickness in four dimensions, and so that two-dimensional universes are measurably thick (even if very thin) membranes to us. Then there might be possibilities for communication.

The parapsychologists might say that mental powers are not limited by dimensional constraints. They might say that astral projection and telepathy can occur in any number of dimensions, and using these techniques, we can communicate with any other beings in all of creation. I would not hazard a guess about those things. I find it difficult enough to believe that these metaphysical phenomena exist at all. I have seen evidence of their reality, some quite astonishing; but never have I seen a solid scientific demonstration of these powers being put to some useful task.

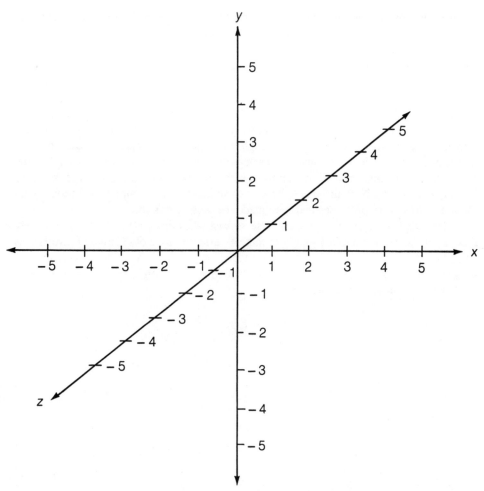

**Fig. 6-9.** The three-dimensional Cartesian system.

## Where's Our Place?

A good subject for conclusion is the question: Where do we fit into the picture of space and time? Why are we here? I won't try to offer any complete answer, but some things come to mind.

First, order can result from chaos in the universe, and we are a highly ordered phenomenon. We are here because the universe is built that way, and chances are excellent that we are not the only form of life in the universe.

Some have said that we are the guinea pigs in a great cosmic battle between good and evil. I doubt that. I suspect those two forces, while real at least by their presence in our minds, are not putting all of their cosmic soldiers right here on this little speck of a planet. How cruel for a "good" force to place us under such stress!

The idea that we are an enduring product of chaos is a reassuring thought. It provides for immortality even if one is agnostic. Look at it this way. Every atom is a product of the chaos of the cosmos, and its order endures for billions of years. The protons, neutrons, and electrons are also ordered, and they have been around almost since the universe began and will be here until the end. In fact, the tiniest particles are almost unalterable. They make up a variety of other things in their total combinations, but they themselves remain the same.

We might think of ourselves as protons, neutrons, and electrons and our universe as, say, a galaxy. The galaxy might evolve, but the fundamental particles remain the same from beginning to end. Each of us is a miniscule being in a vast universe—but that very minuteness gives us lasting power. Although we might not understand it, each of us is interwoven into cosmic reality, just as is each particle of an atom. It is not possible for any single particle of this universe to simply vanish, and the same ought to hold for us as beings, you and me. Not our bodies, which evolve like the stars, but our real selves, who inquire into the very processes that have made the inquiry possible.

The complete knowledge of a universe so vast takes time, a long time. Fortunately there seems to be an unlimited supply of that. A variation of an old Chinese proverb goes something like this: "Even if you don't understand me in a thousand years, you will understand me in a thousand and one years." The time frame might vary, but this is essentially what the universe indicates to us.

# CHAPTER 7

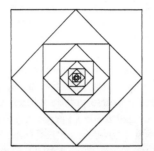

# Partial Dimensions, Fractals, and Mathephysics

IT WAS A SCIENTIST WORKING FOR IBM WHO DISCOVERED A STRANGE GRAPHICAL OBJECT, the representation of a seemingly simple function, that started scientists on mind journeys that carried some away from their careers. The field was some kind of never-never land between mathematics and physics. These two disciplines, while perhaps having some common ground, appear more to be mutually exclusive, with a region between that few, in the past, have dared to tread. Professors and their students were reluctant to publish papers on the subject for fear of rejection by both the mathematicians and the physicists. It was as if some little country could be the enemy of both the United States and the Soviet Union. It was a way of thinking that demanded acceptance of the possibility that some things occur for reasons we cannot know—and in fact can *prove* we cannot know.

Some objects are so complex that they are never resolved despite the degree of magnification. They might have visual irregularities, but a better picture is always expected when they are observed under a microscope. But, alas—the microscope often reveals that there is still complexity as great as or greater than that apparent at the beginning.

This new science, aided by computers, points toward one conclusion: things happen for a mathematical reason, an infinitely complicated reason, and the only way to discover that reason is to look at it as closely as possible. But no matter how close you look, the whole structure of reality can never be exacted because it is infinitely complicated, from the smallest quark to the largest polydimensional "foam" of universes imaginable.

## No Truth Value

In conventional logic, the foundation of all thinking, we usually take for granted that a statement is either true or false. If a contradiction arises—*reductio ad absurdum*—it means there is something wrong with the theory and the axioms must be changed. If the axioms are made too simple or too few, the resulting logical tree will have a trivial structure and will be uninteresting and useless to physicists or mathematicians.

Kurt Godel made an interesting discovery about first-order logic—one of the simplest forms of logic, one that we use in every field of endeavor and daily thought. He found that there are some statements that have no truth value. They are neither provable as true nor provable as false. What is more, Godel *proved* that such statements exist. Thus there are gaps, or holes, in thought of any kind that is based on first-order logic. This is not a quirk of the material world, but a fact about the very fiber of the universe, about the way things are in the deepest cosmic sense.

When something like this happens, a scientist is likely to be scorned. In the academic community, new ideas, especially counterintuitive ones, are met with hostility. No one wants to see their theory of the universe proven wrong. One remarkable astrophysicist, Stephen Hawking, found that he had made an error and that his theory had to be revised. He admitted his error in his book *A Brief History of Time*. Such scholars are rare. Most of them are afraid to admit that they might make a mistake, even though many agree that the universe is so sophisticated that we can only reach closer and closer approximations to absolute truth. This is a paradox: we can never be exactly right, but we can't admit our mistakes!

The Incompleteness Theorem has far-reaching consequences in all realms of thought and reality. First-order logic is the simplest form of logic. More complex forms would contain "holes" in truth, as well. Examples might include statements such as "There is no smallest particle." Is there? Most scientists doubt that it has been found, if it exists. Perhaps it does, and perhaps it doesn't. It will remain unknown unless proof exists either that there is a fundamental particle or that the progression of subparticles and sub-subparticles continues on inward without end. Perhaps it will never be proven. If this is one of the "gaps" in the logical theory of the universe, then it will never be proven. The statement "There is no smallest particle" would thus be neither true nor false.

Such things run counter to most people's way of thinking. Most want to believe that something is either true or it is false. However some things, although addressable in the mind, might actually be unresolvable, even, as it were, by the God that made them.

We do know that the continuum of particles extends downward from the whole known universe, to clusters of galaxies, to individual galaxies and quasars, to stars of all shapes and sizes, to planets orbiting those stars, to asteroids and moons, to mountains and seas, and to life, including man. Further down the scale are cells and crystals, molecules, atoms, electrons, protons, neutrons, quarks, and—well, that's about as far down as we have gotten so far, although there is a plethora of strange particles, some with zero mass, perhaps negative mass, and speeds greater than that of light. The progression could go on without end, *ad infinitum*. Is this true? Or can its truth never be known and, in effect, not exist?

## Particles Without End

The idea that matter is not homogeneous, not a continuous thing but made up of billions of tiny particles, is not new. In fact, matter is mostly empty space. If an object such as a chair could suddenly have all the space taken out from between the particles, it would become so tiny and so dense that it would fall to the center of the earth, cutting like a hot knife through butter. In actual fact, it would fall past the gravitational center of the earth, then return, then fall again, creating a pattern of damped oscillations in a plane or cone as the earth rotated (Fig. 7-1).

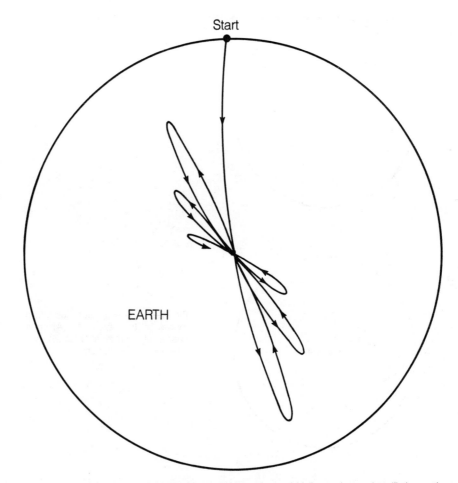

**Fig. 7-1.** A body of extreme density, falling through the earth, would follow a damped oscillating path such as this.

We do know that matter, however complicated its particle structure, does exhibit the property of having a certain, measurable density. The totality of all the particles in an object, however they may be arranged, adds up to something tangible.

It was Rutherford who first developed the idea of atoms, in which negatively charged particles orbited positive nuclei in a manner similar to the way planets orbit the sun. The more dense the material, the greater the number of positive particles in the nucleus, and the more negative particles in orbit around that nucleus (Fig. 7-2 A, B, C). Rutherford's model is considered simplistic to the point of being inaccurate nowadays, and it is an example of how scientific theory refines itself closer and closer to what we hope is the real truth.

Later, scientists found that electrons did not simply orbit the nuclei but existed in spherical "shells" around those nuclei and these "shells" represented the average, or median, position of the electron over a period of time. An electron might in theory stray miles from the nucleus, although this would be highly improbable. Under conditions of

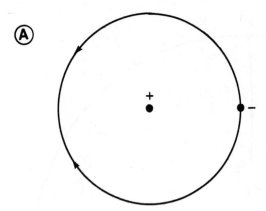

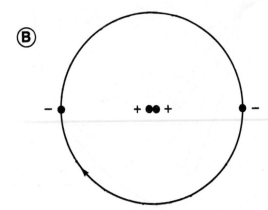

**Fig. 7-2.** The simplified Rutherford model of the atom. At (A), one charge of each polarity; at (B), two charges; at (C), four charges.

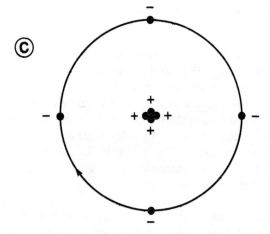

sufficiently high energy, however, electrons sometimes do break free of their nuclei and can wander through space all by themselves, perhaps eventually to be captured by some other nucleus.

Individual protons and neutrons were later found to be made up of subparticles called *quarks*, a term from *Finnegan's Wake* by James Joyce. There were thought to be three kinds of quarks: up, down, and strange. Then more types were found. As if all this is not strange enough!

It is now theorized that there are many other particles. There are *neutrinos*, with zero mass or perhaps infinitesimal mass that can pass through the earth as light through a crystal ball. There are *tachyons*, which supposedly travel faster than the speed of light and for which time goes backwards. There might be antimatter particles with negative mass that annihilate with positive matter if the two come into contact. An interesting development prior to the moon landing was the question: what if the moon is antimatter? Then the spacecraft landing there would have vanished in a fantastic energy display comparable to hundreds of hydrogen bombs. But when the first probe crashed there and no brilliant fireworks erupted in the sky, we knew that the moon was made of basically the same stuff as our own earth.

How many more subparticles will be found? A debate has arisen. Is there a fundamental particle? A particle that cannot be split? A particle consisting of perfectly homogeneous matter? Or does the process proceed down to the theoretical absolute, a geometric point, with no mass and no volume and density thus equal to zero divided by zero, a quantity that is mathematically undefined?

The new science of chaos has revealed that a never-ending sequence of particles could be the reality of the physical universe. This is a place where the mathematician claims his part of the truth: for him, a theory is a structure of its own, a creation of the mind—some would say a simple revelation of what has always been there—and while a mathematical universe might not be much like the physical one, it is reality just as well.

For the mathematician, the complexity of matter with its potpourri of particles and subparticles is of no concern. Most mathematical universes aren't material anyhow. The mathematician's reality is in the mind, beyond the physical, and it can take any form as long as it does not collapse in contradiction or remain vacuous for lack of strength in the axioms. The most extreme, or at least most outspoken, of the mathematicial purists was G. H. Hardy, who expounds his views in his book *A Mathematician's Apology*. The physicist sees a chair as a complex of particles swarming about in a way too complicated to ever fully understand. Even the most powerful supercomputer could not resolve such a structure. The mathematician looks at a chair and says, "Ah! A place to sit and work at my theory!" He then uses tools, often only pencil and paper, to unfold the theory that is built up around his definitions and axioms. The theory might be immensely complicated, and, as Kurt Godel told us, not entirely resolvable, but some of its truths are clear beyond question.

Nonetheless, chaos has invaded the ivory towers of mathematical academe. Computers have aided in the development of a science where the perfection of mathematics exhibits the same baffling impenetrability as the problems of particle physics. Yet chaos is, too, a void between the disciplines.

## Koch Curves, Geometric Dusts, and Other Oddities

Begin with an equilateral triangle (all three sides are the same length and each apex angle is thus 60 degrees) as shown in Fig. 7-3A. Suppose that the length of each side is one unit. Now, trisect each of the sides of the triangle, and take the middle section as the base of an equilateral triangle, forming three new triangles attached to the main one, with sides of $1/3$ unit. Consider the whole figure to be the outer perimeter of this resultant (Fig. 7-3B). Now, again, to each of the 12 sides of this new figure, divide their lengths by three, trisecting them into segments of $1/3^2$ or $1/9$ unit. The middle sections of these sides again serve as the bases for equilateral triangles, and the new figure is the form of the outer perimeter of this (Fig. 7-3C). This process can be iterated again and again to obtain more and more complicated polygons. The polygons look something like snowflakes as the complexity increases. Imagine this process being repeated an infinite number of times. The result is impossible to visualize or draw, but some of its mathematical properties can be evaluated.

This polygon might be called an "infinigon" because it actually has a countably infinite number of sides (countably infinite meaning the number of natural, or counting, numbers). It cannot be resolved no matter how much magnification is applied. It is called a *Koch curve*, named after the mathematician who first described it. Viewed as a whole, it appears as a snowflake-like figure (Fig. 7-4). "Zooming in" on any particular portion of it reveals a certain complicated pattern. But no matter how much magnification is applied, the pattern always looks complicated; even if this curve is magnified a hundred, a thousand, a million, even a googol ($10^{100}$) times, it will still look complicated. Yet it is a very real mathematical object.

The Koch curve has finite area because you can draw a circle around it of finite area and thus know that the area of the Koch curve must be less than the area of the circle. But the perimeter of the Koch curve is infinite. If the initial starting triangle has sides of one unit, then the total perimeter if $3 \times 4/3 \times 4/3 \times 4/3 \times ...$, larger than any real number and therefore aptly considered to be infinity.

Consider a three-dimensional counterpart of this curve. It would be an object with finite volume but infinite surface area. If you could fill up such an object with paint, you would have painted an infinite surface with a finite amount of paint, and, in fact, have used none of that paint in actually coating the surface!

When Helge von Koch first described and demonstrated this mathematical oddity, his colleagues were greatly disturbed. It is counterintuitive to think that an object can have infinite perimeter but only finite interior area. Of course, no such thing could possibly exist in the real world—or could it?

Other mathematicians invented similar bizarre objects. You could begin with a square instead of a triangle and get a progression of figures the first three of which are shown in Fig. 7-5. You could start with a regular pentagon, a hexagon, or any regular or irregular polygon. The result will always be a figure of infinte complexity, finite volume, and infinite perimeter.

An interesting trick, perhaps a way to win money at bars (if you're into using your creative powers to destructive ends), is to draw irregular polygons that are not convex and ask people to look at them for a couple of seconds and then guess how many sides they

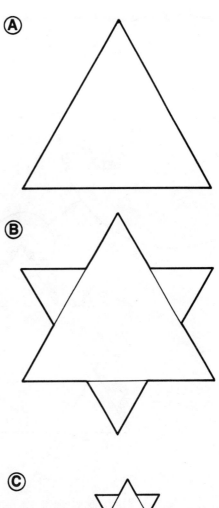

Fig. 7-3. Generation of the Koch curve begins with an equilateral triangle (A). This is then modified as discussed in the text to obtain the figures at (B) and (C). The actual Koch curve is the result of iterating this process infinitely many times.

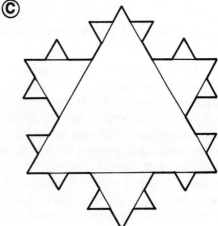

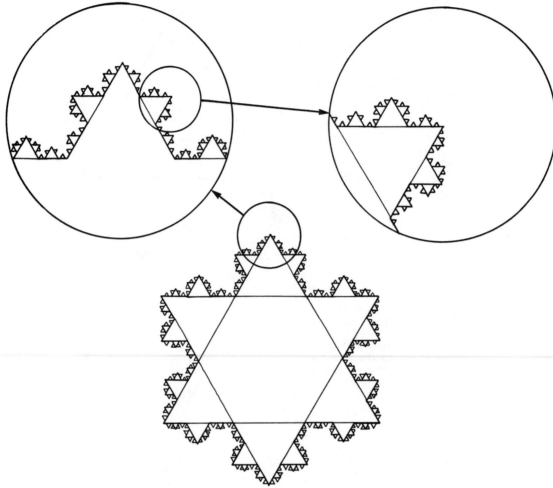

**Fig. 7-4.** The Koch curve appears infinitely complicated, regardless of the degree of magnification. Detail here is limited by the pen point thickness.

have. Examples are shown in Fig. 7-6. The polygons usually have more sides than one would imagine them to have upon casual observation.

Although a Koch curve or similar complex mathematical object cannot be fully visualized, there is a parallel between it and the structure of matter. Material objects are incomprehensibly complicated. The chair you are sitting in is actually a mass of particles, on scales tinier and tinier, perhaps going down to the infinitesimal, and as if this were not enough, the particles are in constant motion.

Another bizarre geometric construction is called a *point dust*. Start with a line segment of some length, such as one unit. Divide the line into some odd number of equal segments, say five. Remove the second and fourth segments, leaving a dotted line that has the same overall length as the original segment but actually just $3/5$ the total overall length. This process is repeated for each of the three new line segments to form a dotted line with

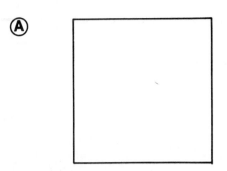

(A)

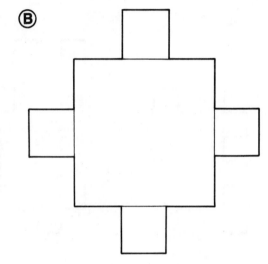

(B)

**Fig. 7-5.** Generation of a figure similar to a Koch curve, but starting with a square (A). The sides are trisected and the middle portion then forms the basis for the added perimeter (B). A second iteration yields the figure at (C).

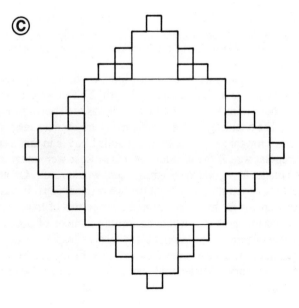

(C)

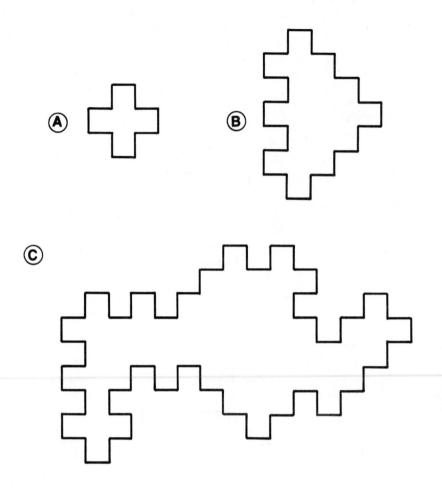

**Fig. 7-6.** Figures can have more sides than a casual glance would seem to indicate. Glance for one second at each of these figures and then count the actual number of sides.

nine ($3^2$) equal parts. The dotted line has the same overall length as the original line but just $3/5 \times 3/5$ of the total actual length. This process is repeated over and over an infinite number of times. The first four iterations are shown in Fig. 7-7.

The total length of the resultant is zero because the product $3/5 \times 3/5 \times 3/5 \times \ldots$ converges toward zero. The resulting dotted line is in fact a set of points, spaced in a certain irregular way. If the iterations of this process were magnified, figures that look the same, no matter how great the magnification, would result. Or, at least, they appear very similar, as long as you stay away from the two original gaps. It was the mathematician Georg Cantor (famous for his research on the properties of transfinite cardinals), who first demonstrated this property, where an infinite number of points, all collinear, could have total length of zero and be impossible to resolve despite the degree of closeness with which it is examined. His ideas were frowned upon by the mathematical establishment, just as was the Koch curve. Matter could not possibly be like that, and the counterintuitive nature of the arrangement caused Cantor to be regarded as some kind of a crank.

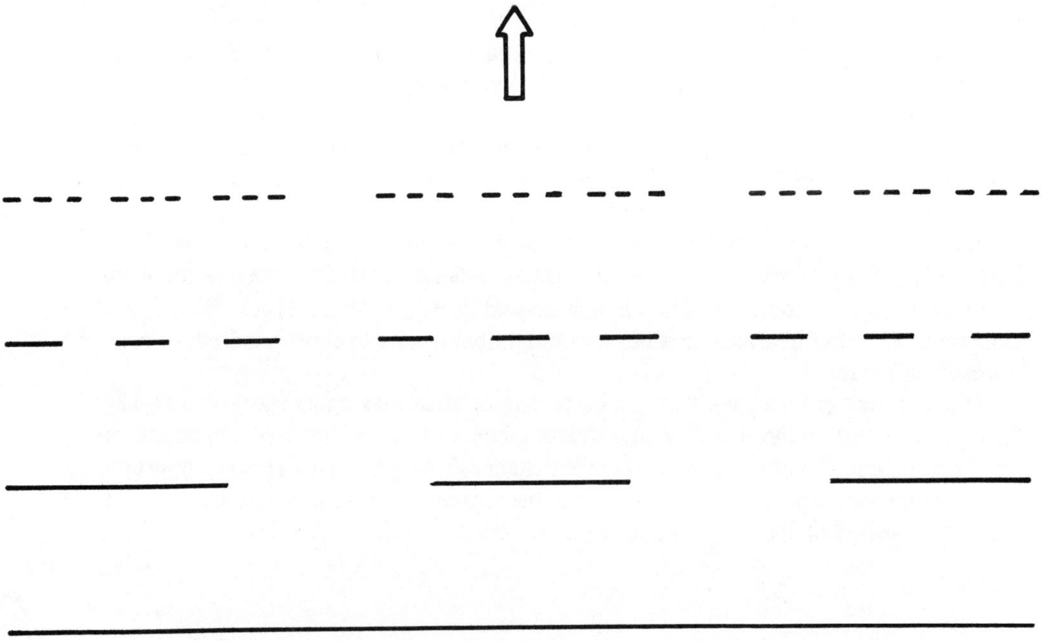

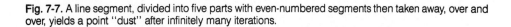

Fig. 7-7. A line segment, divided into five parts with even-numbered segments then taken away, over and over, yields a point "dust" after infinitely many iterations.

Yet is is not difficult to realize that it is possible to take the number line and remove all irrational numbers, leaving only the rational ones, and still have what looks like a continuous line, despite how closely it is examined. The same can be done with the Cartesian plane by removing all of the points having ordered pairs containing irrational numbers. What's left still looks like a plane, no matter how much it is magnified. And this can be done with space by removing any ordered triple that contains an irrational number. The result is still space, a space that always looks perfectly homogeneous no matter how closely it is scrutinized. But the point dusts thus produced are not the same as the point sets in which irrational numbers are included. They are less dense in some mysterious, mind-teasing way. These ideas are simple to imagine and their properties follow with mathematical rigor, but merely talking or writing about them was, at one time, likely to evoke ridicule, scorn, indignation—even anger among one's colleagues.

## The Bug and the Shoreline

The Koch curve and similar mathematical oddities were thought to be merely figments of the purist's imagination. The mathematical world of G. H. Hardy was removed, separate, independent from the physical cosmos, and he preferred it that way. He might not have realized that both his world and the physical world share a common ground, and that the most pure of mathematics can be identical with the most uncertain realities of the physical.

Consider the shoreline of a lake. When I was a child we bought a cottage on beautiful Lac Court Oreilles in northwestern Wisconsin, and my father told me it had something like 57 miles of shoreline. The lake is irregular in shape and is about 6 miles long and 2 miles wide at its widest points. An approximate drawing of the shape of this lake, as it might appear from a satellite 100 miles up, is shown in Fig. 7-8.

But how was this 57 miles of shoreline measured? With a tape measure? A yardstick? A ruler? A micrometer? The lake looks irregular in shape even from 100 miles up—even on a map of the state of Wisconsin. But suppose we zero in on Stukey Bay, in the western part of the lake. Evident are irregularities like miniature peninsulas carved by the waves over the years; there are manmade boat shelter bays; sometimes the exact position of the shoreline is difficult to determine because of grassy, swampy land. Suppose a beetle were to crawl around Lac Court Oreilles, passing around every pebble and rock. Would that beetle travel 57 miles? The answer is no; it would probably have to crawl hundreds or even thousands of miles.

At a still smaller scale, say, that of a bacterium or virus making its way around every single grain of dust on the shoreline, the situation becomes ridiculous. Such an organism would require millions of years to traverse the distance around the lake. This is not just on account of the slow speed and tiny size of the bacterium or virus; it is also because the distance, measured on its scale, would be on the order of millions of miles.

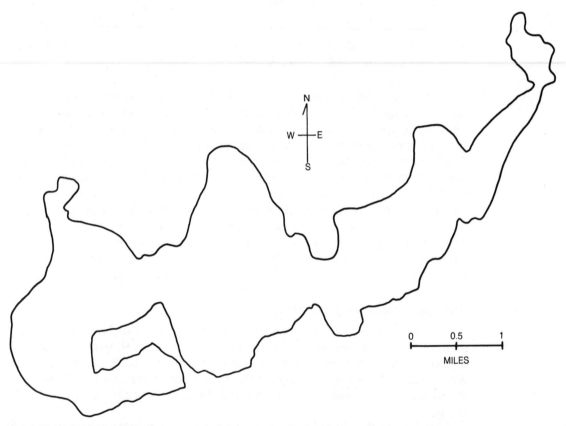

**Fig. 7-8.** Outline of the shore of Lac Court Oreilles in northwestern Wisconsin as shown on a moderately detailed map or as seen from several miles up.

Going yet smaller, bring the scope down to the very atoms themselves, which are made up mostly of empty space anyhow. Imagine ending up going around and around the nucleus of one of the carbon or oxygen atoms. Such travel could go around and around and never get anywhere at all. The distance around the lake would have thus become infinite in the sense that it could not be traversed around solid matter.

The Koch curve, although it is a mathematical peculiarity, is a good representation of physical reality. Its circumference looks finite if examined visually, yet it is infinite. The same is true of the lake in Wisconsin and also the shoreline of any island, lake, pond, or puddle, as well as the coasts of the continents.

There is a difference between the Koch curve and solid matter: the curve in the mathematical sense is continuous in that every point is in some mysterious way connected to every other, but real matter is made up of discrete particles with space in between. This is a physical difference between the imaginary set of points and the actual material as well as a mathematical difference. This might be called a "mathephysical" thing. The two objects represent a never-never land between mathematics and physics. A pure mathematician or physicist might look at us following a discussion such as that just covered and say, "You're talking poppycock. What's the point?" Both disciplines would shun these ideas. It has happened to those who have investigated the nature of chaos, that new science that lies somewhere in between mathematics and physics, having some characteristics of both but being fully accepted by neither discipline.

## Clouds: Tiny, Bigger, Biggest

Clouds and wisps of smoke provide an excellent example of how some things appear the same regardless of scale. The tiny plumes of smoke from a lighted pipe or cigarette are formed by immensely complex patterns of air disturbances. So are the gigantic vortices, fronts, and weather systems characteristic of a low-pressure or high-pressure system in the atmosphere of the Earth. Clouds have the not-so-unique property that they look much the same no matter how close or far away they may be.

I recall flying from Hartford to Minneapolis once and a child remarked of the summer clouds as seen from 30,000 feet: "It looks like water and snow." And it did. It was a perfect description of melting snow in the streets after a severe winter. The dark spaces in between the clouds were the puddles, and the clouds themselves were the melting piles of snow, and they "slushed" together just right.

Clouds look remarkably similar as seen from a satellite hundreds of miles up or as seen from an airplane just a few miles above. The size of the clouds seems to make very little difference. The monotony of the stratus clouds is mimicked by a layer of cigarette smoke in a room where people are sitting around, not moving enough to disturb the layer that has formed. These clouds in turn are similar to the clouds of dust and gas between stars. The scale does not seem to make much, if any, difference.

What is responsible for the cloud patterns visible in the sky on a warm afternoon in June as compared with the wisps of smoke that rise from a candle that has just been blown out? Particles or molecules of different substances, with different refractive or transmission properties for light, are caught up in the turbulence of air. These patterns of turbulence can occur on any scale, from the submicroscopic to the size of the whole atmosphere of the Earth. The exact forces on each atom and the causes for these forces are beyond the capabilities of the most powerful supercomputer to devise—no matter how large or small the turbulence may be. Some try to make predictions based on past experience of what is likely to take place in a few moments, hours, or days for events in the atmosphere of the Earth or predict, quite accurately, that a stellar nebula will appear much the same even after several months have passed. But on large scales of time, large, that is, compared to the size of the event, accurate prediction is virtually impossible. Who knows what the weather will be like at 3:00 p.m. in Chicago on July 20, 2135, for example, other than that it's fairly certain it will be above freezing. No computer analysis is ever likely to resolve that kind of problem. Furthermore, no matter how sophisticated our computers become, there can always be a more complex problem by reducing the size (space) scale or by increasing the time frame.

## Cycles in Nature and Life

There has been much debate recently over the extent to which the activities of man could be changing the global climate. The recent idea is based on the so-called greenhouse effect. Because carbon dioxide, especially, and other byproducts of man's work have increased in the atmosphere in recent decades, and because carbon dioxide acts much as a glass greenhouse when it is in the upper atmosphere, and because there appears to have been a slight global warming in recent decades, scientists are inclined to place the blame for the warming on the increase in the amounts of carbon dioxide caused by man.

This might be an oversimplification. There is evidence of natural climatic cycles that took place long before we ever started to burn fossil fuels. The reduction in the ozone layer over the South Pole and more recently the North Pole as well has been blamed on fluoro-carbons. The fluorocarbons have a capacity for destroying extremely large amounts of ozone. Ozone, the molecule that takes form via the attachment of three (rather than the usual two) atoms of oxygen, is a fragile molecule. It has the property of acting as a natural screen against ultraviolet light from the sun. If the ozone layer in the upper atmosphere were to go away completely, the risk to human and other forms of life would be very great. The primary concern is that skin cancer could become more frequent. However, a drastic reduction in the amount of ozone would pose a threat to the entire ecological balance of the Earth.

There is evidence of upheavals in the past: The sudden disappearance of the dinosaurs is perhaps the most vivid example. Man had nothing at all to do with that. In fact, the dinosaurs had evolved to a degree of natural supremacy in their time that probably sur-passes man's supremacy in our own era. A natural catastrophe of some kind destroyed them all almost at the same time (within a few generations). A natural event, not caused by man, could do the same to us, although we do possess reasoning powers that the dinosaurs did not.

Cycles of drought and over-watering occur. The patterns of climate on our planet are changing all the time. They always have, and, until the sun dies and the Earth becomes a near-absolute-zero ice ball, or until the sun in its red-giant phase burns our planet out of existence, climate always will change. There will be moment-to-moment weather, sea-sonal fluctuations, possible sunspot-related changes, droughts, and famines, as well as times of comparative fruitfulness.

Diseases and epidemics follow similar patterns to those of climate. The plagues of middle-age Europe caused such disturbances that the general distribution of races on Earth has been affected down to this very day. Presently there are diseases that concern us greatly. The Acquired Immune Deficiency Syndrome (AIDS) is a disease of potential not seen since the plagues. It could radically alter the distribution of races and cultures in centuries to come, as compared with what they would be if not for the disease. This particular disease has produced moral consequences that are just in their infancy, as well. Yet, it spreads with a Malthusian curve similar to that of the other diseases. Presumably, better and better methods will be found to control or prevent AIDS, and the injection of such measures into the scenario is eagerly awaited.

But what effect would a vaccination or cure really have on AIDS? Penicillin was invented for such diseases as strep throat and pneumonia, but people still get these diseases and still die from them. There are vaccinations against polio, the childhood crippler that until recently was thought to have been eradicated forever. Yet, there is controversy now about polio. Perhaps a new strain of virus has evolved that is resistant to the vaccine, or is in the process of evolving, or will some day come to be. Viruses are remarkably adaptive to changes in their environment. The AIDS virus is so adaptive that the nickname "voodoo virus" might not be unrealistic. All of these disease-producing life forms are part of a complicated structure, so complicated, in fact, that like clouds, we may never be able to resolve their behavior in predictable ways. They seem to obey structured laws of infinitely irregular detail that fall into the category of the new mathephysics, the new science of chaos.

A vaccine causes an immediate reduction in the number of deaths from a disease if it is an effective vaccine or cure agent. But the long-term eradication of a disease is another matter. Malaria has not gone away despite quinine and mosquito control. Influenza changes its form on an annual basis, and people still die from it. I recall the near-panic over the "swine flu" epidemic in the middle 1970s and President Gerald Ford's campaign of vaccinations. It seemed to me that the vaccine was developed in a hurry and the side effects had not been investigated thoroughly enough. I believed that good health habits would protect me as much as any vaccine in this particular case, and, being just 22 years old and into fitness and good diet, I was probably correct: I would have survived if I had gotten this virus. Nonetheless, almost everyone in my age group got the vaccine. It was almost forced upon the population. The implication was that if you did not get the vaccine, you were flirting with death. (Such is the power of the media!) Only I and another health-conscious fraternity brother in my fraternity did not get it. We were the only skeptics! We did not get the shots, nor did we get influenza. Some people actually criticized us for being irresponsible and for increasing the risk of an epidemic. But to this day, I believe I made the right choice. There *were* complications for some people who got the vaccine. We did not have to fear anything when these potential risks became evident.

Had no one gotten the vaccine, what would have occurred? We will never know, because events occur only once. There will probably be another "swine flu" crisis or similar viral crisis in the next generation, and if people do not get a vaccine then, perhaps the consequences of large-scale vaccine refusal will then be discovered. The science of chaos has provided a glimpse of the long-term effects of a vaccine on a disease such as "swine flu," and the results are enlightening but disturbing: A vaccine does not necessarily (in fact, usually does not) eradicate deaths from a particular disease, but it increases the long-term variability in the number of deaths. The long-term total could in fact *go up*.

In this way, the population curve and the disease curve are similar. A vaccine is like a major crisis in the population of viruses or bacteria that cause the disease in question. The main factor that determines the long-term number of deaths is not the vaccine but the original *r* factor (growth factor) for the agent responsible for the disease. If the *r* factor is small, the number of cases will level off and stay rather constant. That corresponds to a disease such as mononucleosis, a disease not serious, prevalent, or contagious enough to cause the alarm that results in a widespread vaccination schedule. If the *r* factor is larger, a vaccine or antibiotic can be developed; an example of this is strep throat, for which the occurrence is variable between maximum and minimum limits. There aren't any pandemics of this disease, but it always is around, to some extent. The extremely large *r* factor, such as appears to be the case with AIDS, results in a chaotic fluctuation when the critical number of cases is surpassed. A vaccine is like a monkey wrench in a hurricane: it might help temporarily, but the boat will eventually succumb and the monkey wrench itself will sink to the bottom of the sea unnoticed in history. This is not a prognosis of gloom and doom for humanity, but merely a rendition of the way things are, of the structure of reality. Each individual person must, in the final analysis, navigate through the same storm anyway.

Cycles in nature, such as climatic change, are the same way. The activities of man are the monkey wrench. Humans might have some temporary effect on the ozone layer, but if the whole ozone layer evaporates, so will a large part of the cause of it (if the fluorocarbon theorists are right). Large numbers of aerosol-spraying humans will die. Thus will the monkey wrench be lost in the tempest, and the cycle of nature will resume as it would have otherwise. The details may be greatly different at any particular in the long term because of man's temporary intervention, but the pattern will be just the same as far as the science of chaos is concerned. One axiom of chaos is that it is *certain* that instantaneous details are not resolvable—and it doesn't really make any difference.

## Partial Dimensions

Customarily, objects are thought to have a certain integral number of dimensions. A point is zero-dimensional, a line is one-dimensional, a plane surface is two-dimensional. Space is envisioned as being three-dimensional. Why just three dimensions? Why didn't we evolve in two, or four, or six hundred dimensions? Stephen Hawking has a good answer for this in his book *A Brief History of Time*.

Suppose we were two-dimensional creatures. Then how would we digest our food? The alimentary canal would of necessity divide us into two separate parts (Fig. 7-9A). We would break in half. The same would be true for the circulatory system; it is difficult to imagine how blood could flow effectively in a system that would leave our bodies as countless pieces floating around inside a bag of skin (Fig. 7-9B). Hawking argues that life could not evolve under such circumstances.

In a universe with four spatial dimensions, a planet would not be subject to the same gravitational influences. The power of gravitation would be subject to an inverse-cube law rather than an inverse-square law. This would result in planets' orbits being extremely critical. If not almost perfectly circular, the planets would either spiral into the Sun or fly

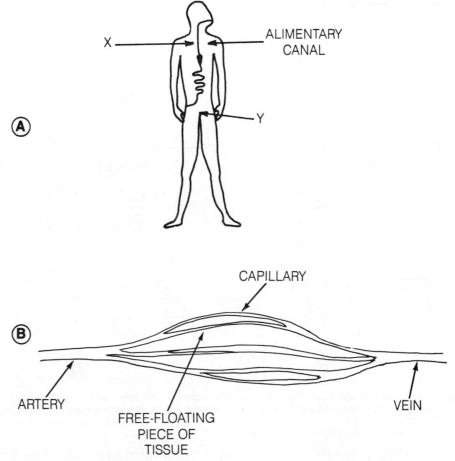

Fig. 7-9. In two dimensions, the alimentary canal would cut a human into two separate parts, here labeled X and Y, as shown at (A). At (B), in two dimensions, a simplified view of capillaries shows how flesh would be broken up into numerous "floating" bits.

off into interstellar space. The slightest perturbing effect would cause either of these two catastrophes to happen, and as a consequence, stars with planets would be extremely rare or nonexistent. Yet, our own Sun in three dimensions supports nine known planets today, and there could be more. Countless asteroids circle the Sun between Mars and Jupiter, and many orbit in sharply elliptical paths without ever falling into the Sun or flying off into space. Binary stars are very common, as well. These would be essentially nonexistent in four spatial dimensions and probably all but impossible in universes having five or more spatial dimensions.

Although dimensions are thought of as being depicted according to the number of coordinates necessary to locate a point, and this means that the number will always be a whole number, in mathephysics there can be exceptions to this. Certain objects could exist in a dimensional never-never land somewhere, for example, between two and three dimensions.

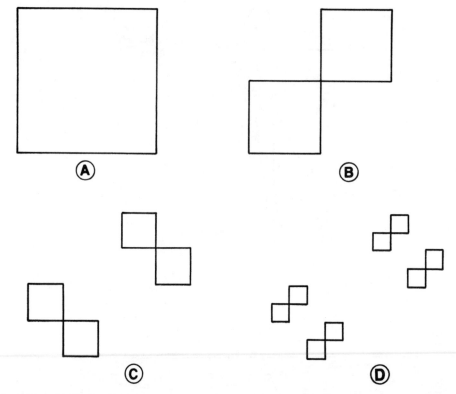

**Fig. 7-10.** At (A), begin with a square; at (B), remove the upper left and lower right squares after dividing the original square into equal quadrants. At (C), the squares at (B) are divided into equal quadrants and then the upper right and lower left squares are removed. At (D), the squares at (C) are broken into quadrants, and the upper left and lower right squares removed.

Consider a square—a two-dimensional object if you consider it and all its interior area on a plane surface. Now divide this square into four equal parts, taking away the upper left and lower right squares in the figure. This is shown in Fig. 7-10 at (A)—the whole square and its interior—and (B)—just two quarters of the square. Repeat this process for the two squares remaining, but this time, remove the upper right and lower left quadrants. The result is in Fig. 7-10C. The next step is to divide the four remaining squares into fourths and perform the original operation on each of them, leaving just the upper right and lower left quadrants (Fig. 7-10D). The total number of squares doubles with each iteration: 1, 2, 4, 8. The number of quadrants into which the original square is divided increases according to the sequence 1, 4, 16, 64, and so on. Thus,

$$S_1 = 2^0, 2^1, 2^2, 2^3,\dots$$
$$S_2 = 4^0, 4^1, 4^2, 4^3,\dots$$

where $S_1$ and $S_2$ represent the number of actual squares and the number of total sections into which the original square has been divided. Also consider D, the density series, as

$$D = S_1/S_2 = (1/2)^0, (1/2)^1, (1/2)^2, (1/2)^2, (1/2)^3,\dots$$
$$= 1, 1/2, 1/4, 1/8,\dots$$

Imagine the figure as it grows in complexity and decreases in density with each iteration. The density series D approaches zero. There is no limit to how small it can get. Mathematicians would say, "Pick any small positive number. Then the series D contains a member smaller than this and still positive." The number of squares increases without limit. Now imagine the end product after an infinite number of iterations as has been described here. The result is a "dust" of points, all within the original square, with zero density but infinite number, and they are in some way connected pairwise. This is because, as you can see by performing the first few iterations, the resultant squares are pairwise connected. They share one point in common per pair, considering the outside boundaries of the squares as parts of each square. The final product occupies two dimensions in that a part of the Cartesian plane is taken up by the points. Yet each "pair" of points is zero-dimensional. How, then, do you define the dimensionality of a set of points such as this?

You might say the set is still two-dimensional since two coordinates are needed for each point. But is this true? Couldn't the squares be numbered in the iteration process such as is shown in Fig. 7-11? They could be all integers or just positive integers, but you could always number the squares. So why not the points? In this sense, the object, after an infinite number of repetitions, is one-dimensional: only one coordinate value is needed for defining each point in the set.

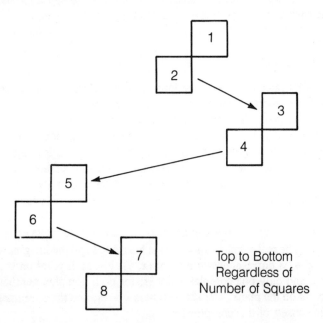

Top to Bottom
Regardless of
Number of Squares

Fig. 7-11. Method of counting the squares at Fig. 7-10D. If they are counted from top to bottom, denumeration is simple no matter how many times the process of Fig. 7-10 (and described in the text) has been repeated.

Say there are a bunch of zero-dimensional objects (points) in a two-space (plane), and they can be defined by integers or rational numbers (that all fall on a number line, a one-dimensional space). How many dimensions are there? It could be debated endlessly. The question is primarily whether there is one dimension or two involved. Say it is a 1.5-dimensional figure. Let's take a vote among mathematicians and physicists. Out of 1,000 people, 589 say that this is a two-dimensional figure and the rest say one-dimensional (there are no "Don't care" or "Don't know" answers here.) Then you could say that the figure has 1.589 dimensions. Certainly it is a complicated process to figure it out—a process that a computer might do in various ways, depending on the programming.

From an ordered and geometrically simple scheme, chaos has been created. It is simply not possible to precisely answer this question beyond any doubt for everyone involved. Mathematics is reduced to a debatable thing, an inexact science. No mathematician likes that! And what physicist is going to allow for the actual existence of a material object like this? Not a single one. Thus we are in that middle ground, thrown out by both disciplines, once again.

Objects having fractional dimensionality are of interest, because in reality, all objects could be of this type. In our three-space, the structure of matter could be such that the progression of smaller and smaller particles is endless. Thus, the surfaces of these particles can be two-dimensional in the sense that the surface of the Earth can be depicted on a spherical globe, but they are three-dimensional because of the myriad surface irregularities. In fact, the surface of an object is so complicated, considering all the individual particles, that it is more than two-dimensional but somehow less than three-dimensional.

## The Mandelbrot Set

Infinitely complicated objects can be formed in other, still simpler ways. Mathematicians and engineers, particularly electrical engineers, are familiar with the Cartesian plane of complex numbers. A complex number is not really any more complicated than a real number; it requires two, not one, parts to depict it. The square root of $-1$ is an unknown and undefined quantity to many "ordinary" people and is often depicted by the lowercase letter $i$. A whole new set of "imaginary" numbers is then formed by the real-number multiples of $i$. A complex number consists of the sum of a real number $x$ and an imaginary number $yi$. Let $c$ be a complex number; then $c = x + yi$, where $x$ and $y$ are real numbers and $i = \sqrt{-1}$.

Complex numbers are traditionally mapped on a coordinate plane called the *complex plane* (Fig. 7-12). The real-number, or $x$, axis is horizontal and the imaginary, or $y$, axis is vertical. Thus, $x + yi$ corresponds to a point $(x, y)$. For each point on the plane, there corresponds one and only one complex number; for each complex number there is one and only one point on the plane. The real numbers $x + 0i$, and the pure imaginaries, $0 + yi$, form special subsets of this complex set.

Take a given complex number—call it $c_0$—and multiply it by itself and then add the result to the original. This results in a new complex number $c_1 = c_0^2 + c_0$. For some complex numbers, this results in a new point farther from the origin $0 + 0i$ than the first point; for some, it results in a point closer in. For some numbers, the distance does not change. Now repeat this process, obtaining $c_2 = c_1^2 + c_1$. Keep going, getting a series of complex numbers $c_0, c_1, c_2, c_3, \ldots$, such that for any $c_n$, there is a new number $c_{n+1} = c_n^2 + c_n$.

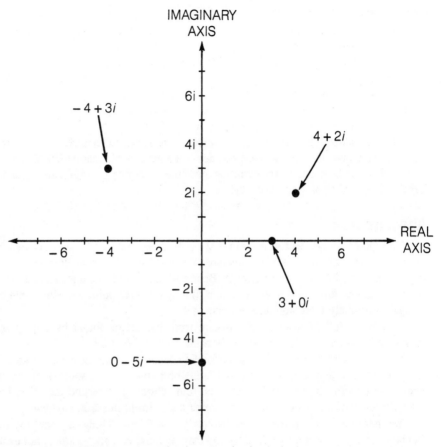

**Fig. 7-12.** The complex coordinate plane, showing several points in the form $x + yi$, where $x$ is the real axis and $y$ is the imaginary axis.

Whether or not this sequence diverges off toward infinity or converges toward zero depends on an unimaginably complicated set of factors. You could map the points on the complex plane into two regions, coloring them, say, black if they converge and white if they diverge. The best, and in fact the only, way to make such a map is via computer, where points are tested one by one. Hundreds, thousands, millions, or more points could be tested on the plane to obtain a finer and finer mapping. As it turns out, this is a necessity, for the resulting pattern is not simple. It evolves at first as a roughly cardioid shape, but as more and more points are tested, "buds" appear on the main form of the mapping.

The line that divides the two regions develops into a set of points having infinite complexity. There are seahorse tails and wavy portions. Regardless of how much magnification is applied—that is, how fine the grid of points in the computer is made to increase the resolution—the pattern never simplifies but keeps repeating chaotically. There are some small shapes that are similar to, but not identical with, the original cardioid pattern. This complex set of points, derived from a seemingly simple but nonlinear function, is called the Mandelbrot set, named after the engineer for International Business Machines, Benoit Mandelbrot, who first discovered it. There are an infinite variety of other such complex sets, but this is the most well-known of them. A home computer can be programmed to reproduce it. Color-enhanced video replications of this set have been sold for money as works of art. This could be called a form of mathephysical art. The Mandelbrot set exists in its entirety but it would require an infinite amount of time to see it all. In fact, the number of years needed to observe all of this set would not be just countably infinite (corresponding to all the integers) but uncountably infinite (corresponding to all of the complex numbers). This would mandate examining each and every point in the complex plane. That's not only impossible, but impossibly impossible.

The Mandelbrot set is of interest because nature seems to be made this way. It is not a physical set of laws that can be resolved, nor is it a predictable mathematical function. Yet with such a simple equation, the resulting structure is infinitely complicated. Such is, perhaps, the very fiber of space and time.

## Absolute Truth

Kurt Godel showed us that even in first-order logic, there are statements for which the truth value cannot be determined. This must also be true of the actual cosmos, which is far more complicated than first-order logic. Benoit Mandelbrot has demonstrated to us how a simple nonlinear formula can result in an infinitely complex point set. The actual universe is, again, infinitely more complicated than this.

Search for full knowledge of absolute truth cannot be found by purely scientific means. What would we do with absolute truth if we did find it?

For those who desire endless pursuit of knowledge, wanting never to know everything, mathematicians like Godel and Mandelbrot ought to be sources of satisfaction. They have proven, the former by rigorous "old school" means and the other by brute-force demonstration, that the chase will never end. Not in this life, anyhow.

Yet there must exist some set of absolutely true things. Things are the way they are. Stephen Hawking was not surprised to find that the universe can "just be," not evolving in the sense of space-time but existing as an entity, complete in itself. We sometimes forget that God is not constrained by time or space.

Einstein once said that God does not play dice with the universe. A few more contemporary theoreticians and experimentalists are saying that perhaps he does. Einstein also said that God might be sophisticated, but he is not malicious. Apparently that is supposed to mean that He doesn't make things complicated in order to be cruel. But there is no doubt that things have turned out complicated. Perhaps they are even more sophisticated than even God ever thought they could be. I suspect that God is not spending all of His infinitely dimensioned "time" looking at the Mandelbrot set or trying to determine the truth values of statements of any sort. Instead, these things must have been allowed to evolve by themselves, so that we, in our own time, might uncover as much or as little of them as we want.

# Index

# Other Bestsellers of Related Interest

## 101 SOUND, LIGHT AND POWER IC PROJECTS—Charles Shoemaker

At last! Here's an IC project guide that doesn't stop with how and why ICs function . . . it goes one step further to give you hands-on experience in the interfacing of integrated circuits to solve real-world problems. Projects include sound control circuits such as alarms and intercoms; light control projects from photoflash slave to a monitor/alarm; power control units and much more! 384 pages, 135 illustrations. Book No. 2604, $16.95 paperback, $24.95 hardcover

## COMETS, METERS AND ASTEROIDS—How They Affect Earth—Stan Gibilisco

Information on meteors, asteroids, and other related space phenomena is all here for the taking. It includes a spectacular eight-page section of color photos taken in space. Packed with little-known details and fascinating theories covering history's most memorable comets—including Haley's Comet—the origins of the solar system, and speculation on what may happen in the future. 224 pages, 148 illustrations. Book No. 1905, $14.95 paperback only

## 333 SCIENCE TRICKS AND EXPERIMENTS—Robert J. Brown

*"Well-described and aptly illustrated."*
—*New Technical Books*

Here is a delightful collection of experiments and "tricks" that demonstrate a variety of well-known, and not so well-known, scientific principles and illusions. Find tricks based on inertia, momentum, and sound projects based on biology, water surface tension, gravity and centrifugal force, heat, and light. Every experiment is easy to understand and construct and uses ordinary household items. 208 pages, 189 illustrations. Book No. 1825, $9.95 paperback, $15.95 hardcover

## VIOLENT STORMS—Jon Erickson

This book provides up-to-date information on recurring atmospheric disturbances. The internal and external mechanisms that cause weather on the Earth and the way these forces come together to produce our climate are examined. Many photographs, line drawings, and tables, as well as a complete glossary make this engrossing book informative, entertaining and easy to read. 240 pages 190 illustrations. Book No. 2942, $16.95 paperback, $24.95 hardcover

---

## Look for These and Other TAB Books at Your Local Bookstore

---

## To Order Call Toll Free 1-800-822-8158

(in PA and AK call 717-794-2191)

### or write to TAB BOOKS Inc., Blue Ridge Summit, PA 17294-0840.

---

| Title | | Product No. | Quantity | Price |
|---|---|---|---|---|
| | | | | |
| | | | | |
| | | | | |

☐ Check or money order made payable to TAB BOOKS Inc.

Charge my ☐ VISA ☐ MasterCard ☐ American Express

Acct. No. _____ Exp. _____

Signature: _____

Name: _____

City: _____

State: _____ Zip: _____

Subtotal $ _____

Postage and Handling
($3.00 in U.S., $5.00 outside U.S.) $ _____

In PA, NY, & ME add
applicable sales tax $ _____

TOTAL $ _____

TAB BOOKS catalog free with purchase; otherwise send $1.00 in check or money order and receive $1.00 credit on your next purchase.

*Orders outside U.S. must pay with international money order in U.S. dollars.*

**TAB Guarantee: If for any reason you are not satisfied with the book(s) you order, simply return it (them) within 15 days and receive a full refund.** BC